WE STOOD
UPON STARS

Praise for
We Stood Upon Stars

"Roger's writing reminds me of Steinbeck's—it brings light to life in the most beautiful and profound ways. After reading this book I want to love my wife, kids, and life more. For that, I am deeply grateful for Roger and this book."

—BRITT MERRICK, pastor, hunter, surfboard shaper

"A poignant travelogue of generations past and present, searching for God in lost places. After reading the first page of *We Stood Upon Stars,* it's obvious Roger's love for adventure and desire to invite everyone else along! I was swept up in 'love like an ocean,' 'grief like a desert,' and 'peace like a river' that flowed through every chapter. From the waves of Ventura, CA, to starlight in the desert, to the taco truck in Marfa, TX, I got lost in the stories of Roger and his family as they learned not only about the beauty of each destination, but the beauty of the journey it takes to get there."

—LESLIE JORDAN, All Sons & Daughters

"It's hard to know if Roger is an author or an artist. He paints these pages with words so vivid and picturesque that you can almost smell the Rocky Mountain air, feel the salty water of the ocean, or experience the tug of a wild trout on the end of a fly line. Roger is writing the powerful story every man, every father, and every adventurer dreams about living, but for Roger it's not a dream. It's his life. And like a wise teacher, he's showing us how it can be our life too."

—BRIAN CARPENTER, founder of Refuge Foundation, Montana

"Roger Thompson takes us on his dirt roads, into his mountains, and deep into his spirit. Through his humor and humility, he will inspire you."

—BRADEN JONES, entrepreneur, world traveler, husband and father, co-founder of Intervals, Petunia Pickle Bottom, Sons of Trade

"There is no better story than one that truly becomes your own. As a guy who finds comfort in security, God is continually drawing me deeper into the unknown . . . and it's good for the soul. In this book, Roger invites us on the road less traveled. *We Stood Upon Stars* is a road map to the journey that every man hopes to experience for himself. Get ready to dive right into the heart of a man."

—GARY HUMBLE, CEO of Grapevine Craft Brewery and blogger at HumbleTravelers.com

"We all search for something in our lives, though many of us are unable to express that. *We Stood Upon Stars* does so—prolifically with love, humor, and solace—'rediscovering a wild that never had been lost.' Beautifully written, must read."

—KynsLee Scott, steelhead and trout fly-fishing guide

"What strikes me most isn't the adventures found within this book, but Roger's transparent ability to share the condition of our human heart. Roger's honest reflections undoubtedly beg us to reflect on our own map and trajectory through life. From finding truth behind VW Vanagon maintenance, to the art of teaching his sons the beauty of fly-fishing, to subtleties of the Creator's whisper on the open road—Roger speaks to the father, husband, and friend who are crafting our own unique maps on this journey."

—RJ Hosking, fellow Vanagon owner, friend, @famwithvan

"*We Stood Upon Stars* is an invitation to adventure . . . permission to explore—both the physical destinations found through travel and the inner places of the heart. Roger warms you up with intriguing (not to mention hilarious) stories, then delivers thought-provoking wisdom at just the right moment. As a mother to four adventure-seeking boys (and married to another one), I know men everywhere will connect with this book as it affirms their dreams, questions, and passions, and ultimately points them to the place where real purpose and meaning can be found."

—Monica Swanson, author and writer at monicaswanson.com

"*We Stood Upon Stars* makes you feel like you are sitting next to a campfire with a best friend, exchanging thoughts and memories of where you've traveled and where you hope to go."

—Kristi Spoon, owner/rancher, Spoon's Rock Creek Ranch

"I've always enjoyed seeing life through Roger's eyes, and now readers get to experience what I have through our friendship for so many years. *We Stood Upon Stars* draws me into beautiful locations, and when I'm not expecting it, Roger drops one of those lines on me that makes me think of something important for the rest of the day. Something eternal. This book is so good for my soul that I can't put it down!"

—Bryan Jennings, professional surfer and filmmaker; founder
  of Walking on Water

WE STOOD UPON STARS

FINDING GOD IN LOST PLACES

ROGER W. THOMPSON

WATERBROOK

WE STOOD UPON STARS

Details in some anecdotes and stories have been changed to protect the identities of the persons involved.

Trade Paperback ISBN 978-1-60142-959-9
eBook ISBN 978-1-60142-960-5

Cover design by Kristopher K. Orr; cover photography by Joshua Stutzman
Interior art by Elain Thompson and copyright © Elain Thompson and Roger Thompson

Published in the United States by WaterBrook, an imprint of the Crown Publishing Group, a division of Penguin Random House LLC, New York.

WATERBROOK® and its deer colophon are registered trademarks of Penguin Random House LLC.

Library of Congress Cataloging-in-Publication Data
Names: Thompson, Roger W., 1972- author.
Title: We stood upon stars : finding God in lost places / Roger Thompson.
Description: First Edition. | Colorado Springs, Colo. : WaterBrook, 2017. | Description based on print version record and CIP data provided by publisher; resource not viewed.
Identifiers: LCCN 2017001219 (print) | LCCN 2017011692 (ebook) | ISBN 9781601429605 (electronic) | ISBN 9781601429599 (pbk.)
Subjects: LCSH: Thompson, Roger W., 1972- | Christian biography—United States. | Travel—Religious aspects—Christianity. | United States—Description and travel.
Classification: LCC BR1725.T465 (ebook) | LCC BR1725.T465 A3 2017 (print) | DDC 277.3/083092 [B]—dc23
LC record available at https://lccn.loc.gov/2017001219

Printed in the United States of America
2017—First Edition

10 9 8 7 6 5 4 3 2 1

SPECIAL SALES
Most WaterBrook books are available at special quantity discounts when purchased in bulk by corporations, organizations, and special-interest groups. Custom imprinting or excerpting can also be done to fit special needs. For information, please e-mail specialmarketscms@penguin randomhouse.com or call 1-800-603-7051.

To my boys of whom I am proud.
Hayden and Austin, may your lives be full of
adventures that one day become legend.

Contents

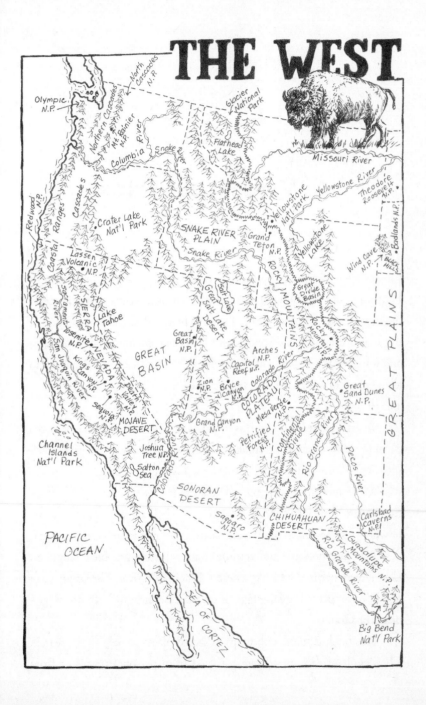

THE WEST

A Word About Maps

I make a lot of wrong turns. They come easily. A slight distraction or curiosity and I'm down a washboard road rattling my van and teeth, making for a distant landmark. The turns come after full consultation of the maps. I'll study the topography for hours, memorizing mountains and watersheds. I'll glance at the roads as well, but I've traveled enough to know roads of men can't always be trusted. It's better to trust in immovable things.

We make our homes in this world as best we can. We scratch at the earth to make a living or to make a difference, and always we have a feeling there is something more. Something missing. So we search.

We search mountaintops and valleys, deserts and oceans. We hope sunrises and long views through canyons will help us discover who we are or who we still want to be. We also search our own inner landscapes and describe our emotional and spiritual state with topographical language. Love like an ocean. Grief like a desert. Peace like a river. The language of our hearts reflects the language of creation because in both are fingerprints of God.

This book is filled with maps of sacred places to help in the search. The details of each map were gathered from personal travels or from those of close friends. They lead to secret shorelines that will deepen our love for our wives and to rivers where we cast a line with fishing buddies who, through wild trout and campfires, will become enduring friends. These maps lead to distant lakes where in safety we can cry out our hopes and shames and hear mountains echo with assurances that we are not alone.

Individually these maps propose specific adventures throughout the West. They highlight fishing holes and wilderness and the best breweries to help cap the day. Collectively these roads through the wilderness present the map of a man's heart.

While traveling I'll often veer onto a road that wasn't on my route. This is the beginning of adventure. It's how I've discovered tiny towns and sunsets and secret fishing holes and the Philipsburg Brewing Company in Montana. It's also how I've gotten myself desperately lost. And since it takes an act of Congress to get me to turn around, I keep going over switchbacks and single-lane roads until either the curiosity is cured or I run out of snacks. Before turning back I get out and survey the landscape, looking to mountain peaks or rivers or stars for clues. It's always there, deep in the wilderness, with my wife or my kids or my buddies or alone, where—in desperation for answers or simply curiousity—I am met by God.

My hope is these stories and maps will help you with your own adventures and discoveries. That you'll go to the edge of your known world. Then a little beyond. And that in lost places you'll find what it is you're searching for.

Travel well,
Roger

JOSHUA TREE
NATIONAL PARK

MARINE CORPS AIR GROUND COMBAT CENTER

18
247
18
247

0   10   20
MILES

Deadman Lake

BIG BEAR LAKE
- Bear Mountain Ski Resort
- Snow Summit Ski Resort
- Summer Water Sports
- Standup Paddleboarding

Poppy & Harriers

38

Joshua Tree for the People (pizza)
Pie for the People (pizza)
Joshua Tree Coffee Co.
Noah Purifoy Outdoor Desert Art Museum

Twentynine Palms
Jelly Donut

SAN BERNARDINO MOUNTAINS

Pioneer Town
Old West Town
good live music
& BBQ

YUCCA VALLEY

62

"Dark Sky" Star gazing

Key View

JOSHUA TREE NATIONAL PARK

Pinto Basin Road

Fun Dinosaurs at Cabazon

62

79

243

COACHELLA

10
Ernest Coffee
La Quinta Brewing Co.
Palm Springs

111

Take Gondola to top of San Jacinto Peak

74

Idyllwild

SAN JACINTO MOUNTAINS

111
Indio

Coachella

VALLEY

866

74

PALM SPRINGS & Surroundings
- Hike Palm Springs Indian Canyon Trails
- Sparrows Lodge & Kora-Kia for romantic couples retreat
- Martinis at the Tennis Club bar for old-school Palm Springs experience
- Road trip to quirky Salvation Mountain
- Burgers at Ski Inn
  ↳ Lowest bar in Western hemisphere

86

Box Canyon Road

SALTON SEA

111
Ski Inn

Salvation Mountain

1

The Light That Has Always Been

Joshua Tree National Park, California

I live on the western edge of the continent, under the storied shadows of great men. And I wonder if I ever can become one of them.

Grandpa rode out of the Oklahoma dust bowl on the back of a Harley Davidson after the Great Depression. His father, my great-grandfather, was driving. To make better time, his father tied Grandpa to his body with a rope so Grandpa could sleep without falling off. Though in oven winds, sleep seldom came.

The motorcycle's engine labored as it bled gasoline from the carburetor, acrid air smelling of metal and burnt fuel. The heat rose from volcanic depths of the Earth, radiating through an endless strip of tar laid by desperate men working government projects to put meat in the bellies of their children. The wind brought no relief, nor did the night. For days they traveled, through sand and bleached-bone deserts, bound to one another and bound to a hope that things would be better in the West.

The Harley Davidson 45 was a workingman's bike, within reach of even a Depression-era preacher such as my great-grandfather. The leather seats still smelled of farmyards near where the Harley was built, and the flathead engine was the most dependable design of any bike its age. Even when something would go wrong, an owner with a basic set of tools and an average knowledge of engines could repair it. In this way it was most American.

The heart of the flathead beat through valves in a sideways rhythm, giving the bike a slight tremor as the two rode west. Accompanied only by engine noise and thought and sounds of a wind, it seemed they had all of America to themselves. And with nothing separating them from the heat and the dust, the motorcycle, carrying two bodies bound together, became one with the landscape.

In the wide flat of desert, smells provided the first sign of things to come. A dead animal could be smelled long before it was spotted. Bacon on the skillet promised a café where men with cracked skin gathered over coffee in cracked mugs. When talk turned to rumored rain, the voices would lower, either out of reverence or fear of scaring it off.

These were days of struggle, the highway a string held taut between opposing troubles. To the east lay desolate farmlands and cities crushed by economic collapse. To the west lay the relocated desperation of migrating people.

Millions of ragged souls were led not by fire or cloud, but by hunger and hope in the promises of the West. For most, the promises would prove false. The migrants would arrive to dreamed-of opportunities that had evaporated. Grandpa once told me Okies were the Americans hardest hit by the dust bowl and the Depression. Landowners were eager to exploit the endless supply of cheap Okie labor, and Californians hated them for their feral appearances—their bodies carved by starvation and the lack of basic essentials, such as water for bathing. Law keepers feared them because of their sheer numbers.

My great-grandfather prayed for the hungry and the desperate with his fists clenched on handlebars and teeth gritted to keep the dust from his lungs. He knew them well from his years spent preaching in the Oklahoma Panhandle. And they knew him because he had become one of them. He lived at the same level of poverty, raising his family in converted chicken coops and trailers perched on cinder blocks. He preached in several brush-arbor churches on the same day, traveling miles from one to the next, being paid with nothing more than half a bag of vegetables gleaned from the skeletal farms of those who came to hear him.

With his son now tied to him, he sped west. There, desperate people would need to know the same hope he preached in the dust bowl. Though this highway-like life may connect struggle to struggle to struggle, there is a final destination—an eternal life without struggle in a land without dust and death.

When my great-grandfather arrived in California, he would build a church and tell this to anyone who would listen.

$$\times$$

The great deserts of the West—the Mojave, the Sonoran, the Great Basin—funnel travelers into Southern California through a pass between two great mountain ranges. The San Jacinto Mountains to the south and the San Bernardino Mountains to the north rise higher than ten thousand feet and greedily capture any remaining moisture from the Pacific Ocean. The towering ranges ensure that rain does not reach the deserts to the east, where one could die of thirst in sight of mountain peaks covered with snow. The mountains reminded travelers moving through the pass that most of what they hoped for lay just beyond their reach. Many would return home once the great illusion of the West stripped them of all that remained—their dwindling money, their hopes, their human dignity.

It was here, between the desert and the hope, that my great-grandfather built his church. He and my grandfather found a place to build in the unincorporated area of Cabazon, California, located in the pass between the mountains. Money was scarce. A good offering at a church service might consist of bread baked by a family that had received an extra ration of flour or wheat. So Great-Grandpa preached under a tent, and my grandfather went to work for a concrete-block company outside the young resort town of Palm Springs. While movie producers and starlets lounged around newly built swimming pools, Grandpa spent his teenage years mixing cement and water with the more unbearable elements of the desert—sand, gravel, and heat. He formed into molds the very thing he was trying to escape. Through toil he transformed the desert, breaking its will, turning it into something human.

The sun worked behind him, baking the molds and baking his neck and arms. Since there was no money, the concrete company let him keep every fourth block so he could build his father's church. As he mixed concrete and baked blocks, he looked past the desert and the mountain pass gateway to the interior of a golden California where anything seemed possible. Shortly after completing the church building, he would move on to find his purpose. Continuing farther west, he would build a life for himself and his family for generations to come.

In the morning, my wife, sons, and I pass the site where my great-grandfather's church once stood on our way to Joshua Tree National Park. I tell my boys about their great-grandfather and their great-great-grandfather, and they wonder how the world could ever have been so cruel. My head filled with thoughts of motorcycles and desert heat, and I yell at my boys to stop playing with the windows so the perfectly cooled air won't escape. They go back to watching movies or playing video games. I go back to enjoying music and my iced latte, and I wonder if I would have tied them to me on a motorcycle or if I would have just given up and starved to death somewhere near Amarillo, Texas.

We continue our journey to Joshua Tree because I want my boys to understand something about where they come from and because, after years of running from the shadows of men in my life, I'm now running toward them. I am hoping for shadows to become a cover of cloud to guide me through the desert.

I have been running for fear of being defined by my history or finding that I never will measure up to it. But you can't outrun your own story. Only with the hard pruning of time can you edit it and rewrite the ending.

Like most of the Gen X generation, I didn't know anything about Joshua Tree National Park until U2 recorded an album with the title *Joshua Tree*. In my youth I drove through the desert with windows down and music up and asked questions that reached the stars. And oh, the stars. They lit up the night sky, hanging so low it felt like I was driving through light from heaven. I've tried often to recapture that feeling, but some feelings are meant for a specific time and cannot be reclaimed.

I tell this story to my sons.

"Dad, that's boring. When are we going to get there?"

Joshua Tree National Park is a rock-climbing paradise. People come from all corners of the world, working their fingers into cracks in the rock to ascend desert walls and touch the eternal. We arrive to greetings of chalk-handed climbers equipped with ropes and shoes to wedge into split rock. Though we have none of this, there are plenty of boulders for us to climb and explore.

We camp in Hidden Valley, nestled among rocks the size of buildings. As if we've discovered an ancient city, we search the boulevards and alleyways connecting neighborhoods of stone. But upon further inspection, the boulders seem more alive. The strata give each formation a depth and personality. Some have weathered storms well. Others have been eroded by wind and rain. Still they sit, as they have since the first mornings of Earth. Today they tell us stories of weather and of those who wander the desert.

The travelers who didn't come here for climbing came for the stars. We are wired to look up, to seek the dark sky and wonder what is out there and where it all came from and what our purpose is in it. The stars direct even the compass. And the clarity of the desert is the best place to look and to seek. Sometimes being lost in the desert is the closest we'll be to finding our way. About 10 percent of the Earth is covered by desert. Perhaps our lives should reflect the same.

The Joshua tree itself looks tormented. Angular branches twist and contort, the limbs desperately rising toward the sky. At the end of each limb is a collection of long spiked palms that resemble a character from a Dr. Seuss book. Legend has it the Joshua tree was named by early pioneers who wandered west looking for a place to build a better life. In their search they came upon a strange tree with limbs raised to the sky, which they thought resembled the upstretched arms of Joshua, leading people into the Promised Land.

Men always have sought the West. Westward movement has provided purpose, drive, and opportunities to achieve greatness. Now the American West is done. Even the mountains and deserts have been gentrified, the rugged edges dulled. The land has been settled and businesses, schools, and churches built. And men are better at building churches than attending them. Now, with streets mapped and towns gridded and cars and phones outfitted with GPS, men seem more lost than ever. What purpose can men find when there is no more West to conquer? What greatness can they achieve?

Most people live in cities that grew from the visions of men whose names are plastered on street signs and buildings. I've looked at the buildings and have wondered how my name will be remembered. And I have tried to look beyond, to the stars and my youthful clarity of driving streets that have no name. But few stars can be seen from the city. There is too much man-made light. A false light. Now the questions asked no longer reach to the stars; they reach only as far as city lights allow. Without the stars there is no way to double-check the accuracy of the compass.

In the desert there is only the light that has always been. And in descending darkness, stars fall upon us. I am surrounded by heaven and stand like Joshua, silent, with arms raised. The stars demand bigger questions. Something within us prompts us to ask, yet the stars do not answer—at least not right away. They return our questions to the heavens where they gather with all questions asked in the dark and reappear in some future night as a star to help navigate the way.

As our last night at Joshua Tree National Park begins and my boys and I search for a path back to our campsite, an answer emerges. My kids don't need the greatness that comes with building buildings and traveling to settle in the West. My boys think I'm great just because I'm here with them. Between unnamed boulders and boulevards, I realize a new name has been given to me. It will be known only by two, and that is purpose enough.

"Dad."

"What?"

"Where are you going? The campsite is this way."

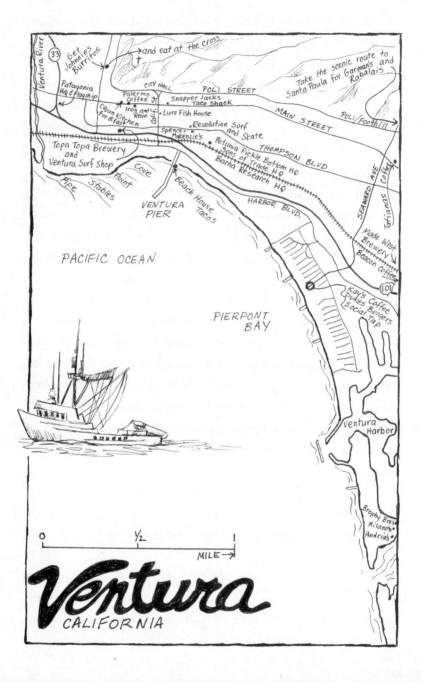

Get
Johnnies
Burritos

→and eat at the cross
†

Ventura River

33

Patagonia
HQ & Flagship

CITY HALL

POLI STREET

Take the scenic route to
Santa Paula for Garmans and
Rabalais

Palermo
Coffee

Snapper Jacks
Taco Shack

Cajun Kitchen
for B'fast

Iron and
Resin

Calif St.

Lure Fish House

MAIN STREET

Poli/Foothill

Topa Topa Brewery
and
Ventura Surf Shop

Spencer
Makenzie's

Revolution Surf
and Skate

Petunia Pickle Bottom HQ
Sons of Trade HQ
Barna Research HQ

THOMPSON BLVD.

SEAWARD AVE

Tuffano's Coffee

Point

Cove

Pipe

Stables

Beach House Tacos

VENTURA
PIER

HARBOR BLVD.

101

Made West
Brewery

Beacon Coffee

PACIFIC OCEAN

PIERPONT
BAY

Kay's Coffee
Dukes Burgers
Social Tap

Ventura Harbor

Brophy Bros
Milano's
Andria's

0   ½   1
                    MILE →

Ventura
CALIFORNIA

2

Hometown Ghosts

Ventura, California

The squid boats arrived in the dark. Metal hulls sat high above docks where men cleaned and scrubbed and fought against effects of the sea. Through the night, they lowered frameworks of stadium lights over the water, attracting squid to the surface to be caught in massive nets. Men set out from the ships in skiffs to surround a shoal of squid. They checked the floats and the knots. The knots must hold.

Ships worked the channel between the mainland and the islands that make up Channel Islands National Park, one of the least visited in the country. These small land masses are often referred to as the Galápagos of the Northern Hemisphere. They remain mostly untouched, a reminder of the Eden this land once was. In the shadows of the islands, boats made their catch and then set their compass home.

I woke before the sun to go surfing. Water is darkest predawn, in the placid hours prior to the shifting of winds. The only sounds were waves and foghorns and distant rumblings of a night train. While the city slumbered, the harbor was alive with motion and the smell of squid. Vacuums sucked the large-eyed creatures from bellies of hulking vessels and dumped them from conveyer belts into wheeled tubs of ice. The squid then were loaded aboard semitrailers and transported to nearby plants to be frozen and packaged and shipped to China. In local restaurants, the mantles and tentacles would be cut and fried and served as fresh calamari. The men worked in silence, fueled by black coffee in stainless-steel thermoses and thoughts of sunrise.

I am in the middle of a long and complicated relationship with Ventura, California. I was born here, so we always have known each other. I know that the early-summer sun is slow to burn through the fog, and no matter how much I might wish for snow, Christmas often is the warmest day of the year. And Ventura knows me: hopes and heartbreaks that over the years I've brought to its hillsides and shores.

As I've aged, the relationship has changed. The land has given as it has taken. It has given romantic spots for a first love and a first kiss, secret surf breaks to explore with buddies, and a niche in the harbor where I started my first business with my best friend, Tim. (It was a surf-clothing company called South Jetty, named after a surf spot formed from what then was the last jetty in town.)

South Jetty is where I confided in Tim about girls and struggles and the death of my father. I was baptized here at south jetty, as were my kids. And when Tim died, the boat passed the jetty before spreading his ashes at sea. I return often to visit the ghosts.

I surfed the jetty at dawn, passing the harbor where fishermen unloaded their catch. Their work is long and hard. Once the catch is unloaded, the men will spend the money they earn in local cafés. Their orders will be taken by single mothers or at times by surfers who save their tips for their next big trip. The food will be cooked by immigrants who send money to family members living in Mexico.

Ventura is a working-class town. It's devoid of universities and large corporations and the cultural strata those institutions create. Everybody here is on an equal level. It's a culture of common respect—for our work, for our resources, for one another. Ventura is a place where doctors surf with high school dropouts. There are no box seats to the opera.

For this reason Ventura has been given names such as Ventucky and Bakersfield by the Sea. You notice a few of the reasons in an overabundance of thrift stores and sketchy tattoo and massage parlors. Ventura also has been called a haven for hippies and the homeless. The public restrooms often smell like weed.

But this is not Ventucky. For those of us fortunate enough to have grown up here, Ventura is more like the deep tracks of a favorite record album. Not the flashy singles meant for popular consumption, but the artful melody embodying the heart of the artist. This town is made up of songs that move a soul.

Ventura is bound geographically between mountains and the ocean. It is further outlined by two rivers. Its city limits are hemmed in by fields known for having some of the most fertile topsoil in the country, growing strawberries and avocados, celery and lemons. The fields keep the city honest. Any expansion of the city requires a tradeoff of produce for concrete.

The city is nestled banana-like along coastal foothills that are barren of trees with the exception of a single hill that boasts two eucalyptus trees at the top. On the hill farthest to the west, only a stone's throw from the ocean, sits a wooden cross. It was erected by the padres, founders of the California missions. Since the establishment of Ventura's mission in 1782, the cross has served as a guidepost for travelers, alerting them to the existence of a mission. It's also a great place to make out.

This land has been occupied for thousands of years. The Chumash

Native American people were here long before the Spaniards and their missions. The Chumash were known as bead makers or "seashell people." They had no need to travel with the seasons or to follow game for food. The Chumash were water people, looking to the ocean. They made seafaring canoes that allowed them to travel easily between communities on the islands and to fish for deepwater game. The easy access to ocean and fresh water and year-round mild temperatures made this area one of the most resource-abundant places on Earth. As a result, the Chumash were a mellow, happy tribe.

This mellow vibe is felt today. We are still water people. The Ventura shoreline curves so that its northernmost and southernmost beaches extend like tips of a crescent moon. In between live the stories of our people. Mine began with troubles. I went to the water's edge and gave them to the Maker of the ocean, where they were tumbled with the tides and given back as something beautiful. Like a piece of sea glass from a long-ago-discarded bottle.

The town is nuanced. Yes, it has too many thrift stores and the rest. But it also has great taco shops and artists and a coffee roaster who sources coffee directly from farmers because the quality is higher and it's the right thing to do. People in Ventura look after one another. In these ways perhaps Ventura does set itself apart from other Southern California cities.

Individually. Together. We gather at the crescent edge of the sea to walk along the wooden pier or on wet sands between the jetties. We look to the ocean expectantly. There must be something in the water.

The temperature at the beach is coldest when clouds sit heavy on the hillsides. When they clear, often following a cold rain, snow can be seen on the mountains beyond. The wind curves over the eight-thousand-foot peaks of the Los Padres National Forest and funnels through a series of descending valleys before reaching the water. In its descent, the wind picks up speed and carries a cold that penetrates even the toughest Patagonia fleece jackets designed in the company's headquarters just up the beach. Suiting up to surf in early spring can feel like getting ready for an expedition to the arctic. Four-millimeter wetsuit. Thick booties. A hood. The water bites through it all.

From the water I look back on my hometown. I can see the ghosts. I hold them like shadows I can't let go of. My best friend, Tim. My dad. The land where I buried broken pieces of my heart. I've run from here, thinking I could escape the past. I built a new life in another town, thinking Ventura was holding me back. I've cursed Ventura. I've been embarrassed by Ventura. Some days the town looks like it woke up and decided to go through the day in sweatpants and slippers.

In my running I've traveled the great cities of our country and other countries. Inevitably, with the benefit of distance, I would think of Ventura and my hometown ghosts. While exploring hill towns in southern France, the nuanced Mediterranean light reminded me of the pink moment back home, just before the twilight, when the last light of day is caught between the Topatopa Mountains and peaceful Pacific waters. It's a moment when time and distance are held in the subtle beauty of a world as pink as a rose. From wherever I'd gone I would return, more enchanted than when I left.

Land has a hold on us. Hometowns are the earth in which we are planted. We take root and grow with the rain and sun given. Some hometowns are a good earth, rich and fertile. Others are a desolate soil where nothing good can grow. We've bled on our land. Falls from skateboards and bikes and noses bloodied when defending childhood honor. Our blood mixes with the dirt and becomes something stronger, glue that binds us to a place. We will defend that place, at times to our own deaths. When a foreign dictator threatens our peace, farmers and schoolteachers become soldiers. When airplanes knock down our buildings, we declare our land holy and rise to defend it. Throughout history, nothing has been fought for so vehemently as land. It is because the dust under our feet defines who we are.

We all have complicated relationships with our hometowns. The place we're born says something about our family. If we stay, or leave, it says something about us. A town has a narrative that is difficult to escape. Even Jesus was dismissed because of his hometown. "Can anything good come from Nazareth?"

At some point we all desire to be a kite, to soar at heights that allow us to be all we are capable of being. To look down and recognize our towns and ourselves differently. No longer defined by family or neighborhood friends or old girlfriends or boyfriends or those awkward junior-high years or by what happened or didn't happen in high school. These are the easy definitions, but they aren't the right ones. We can break free. Go to college. Chase a love. Explore the world. We can choose to soar. When we do, we anchor kite strings to our hometown. Not to tether us to our past, but to let us know how far we've flown.

I walked the beach in fleece-cold mornings of spring. In a lowering tide I made first steps in uncertain sand between water and earth. I started at the last jetty and continued south. It's still called "new jetty" by those of us who remember the old currents. The dunes shift with history. Girlfriends and fistfights in bonfire days of high school. Dreams and careers in the full-moon tides that raise all boats. Baptisms. Marriages. Births. Deaths. These are the footprints in the sand. I walk in the comfort of my history with this land. To grow here, to leave and come back, is a making of peace. I am a product of Ventura, California. My history here is woven as tightly as a squid-boat net. With only good, or only bad, cords hang neatly but remain useless. The knots in life are what create strength.

We all have our peace to make. As much as a hometown comforts, it also wounds. It haunts like a first love. The childhood that never felt like a childhood. The loss of someone cutting to the very core of our history. Of who we are. The standing alone in desperation of darkness, begging for a light that never came.

Our hometowns are lands of *could haves* and *should haves*. These are the wounds that run deepest and the reasons most people leave. But there is no distance we can travel where a childhood smell carried on a distant breeze won't take us immediately back to our hometown. We can run from our ghosts, but it's better to let them go.

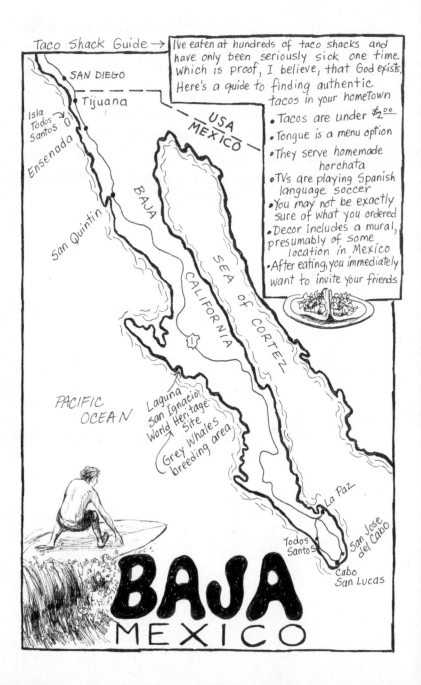

Taco Shack Guide →

I've eaten at hundreds of taco shacks and have only been seriously sick one time. Which is proof, I believe, that God exists. Here's a guide to finding authentic tacos in your hometown

- Tacos are under $2.00
- Tongue is a menu option
- They serve homemade horchata
- TVs are playing Spanish language soccer
- You may not be exactly sure of what you ordered
- Decor includes a mural, presumably of some location in Mexico
- After eating, you immediately want to invite your friends

SAN DIEGO
Tijuana
USA
MEXICO
Isla Todos Santos
Ensenada
BAJA
San Quintin
SEA of CORTEZ
CALIFORNIA
PACIFIC OCEAN
Laguna San Ignacio World Heritage Site
(Grey Whales breeding area)
La Paz
Todos Santos
San Jose del Cabo
Cabo San Lucas

BAJA
MEXICO

3

Problema Grande

Northern Baja, Mexico

The guys with machine guns may have prompted the question.

"Have you been here before?"

"No."

"Do you know where we're going?"

As with all things in Mexico, the answer left room for negotiation.

"Of course I do."

Erik and I crossed the border before midnight under sheets of rain. Friends said they'd be camping at a place called Shipwrecks, and we couldn't resist the idea of spending spring break in uncrowded surf. They had provisions; we just had to get there. But now we were stopped at a border checkpoint surrounded by guys with guns.

The leader spoke in broken English. "Why you here?"

He leaned against our truck with one hand on the machine gun's trigger and the other holding the muzzle. His mustache hadn't fully grown in. Since I had taken two years of Spanish, Erik elected me as interpreter.

"El surfo?"

The gunman studied us while his comrades poked our bags and the surfboards with their weapons. We had been warned that the border patrol might ask for bribes, but these guys looked like night-shift trainees. They waved us through the entry point, and I gave Erik the few details I had.

"We take the highway that's closest to the ocean for four hours, and we'll see a sign that says SURF. When we get to the beach, there'll be a big ship that's wrecked."

"Okay," he said, then added, "If we don't find them, let's drive to the tip of Baja."

"Okay."

Night is darker when you're in unfamiliar places. The darkness could be felt through cracks in our windows. Heavy. Convincing. As a shield from fear, we listened to tapes of R.E.M. and The Replacements. We drove deep into the hours between night and dawn, when nothing stirs and nothing good can happen. Four hours later there was no SURF sign. There were no signs at all.

A single light appeared on the horizon, and we approached it like moths. It was hanging from the awning of a gas station with a dirt driveway in front. The awning was rusting, and only one gas pump worked. We were near the town of San Quintin, which meant we had driven too far. Dawn would soon break, so instead of searching for a SURF sign, we parked behind the gas station and slept.

We awoke to the sounds of chickens and noticed that kids were searching the truck bed for anything useful.

"Chicle! Chicle!" they yelled, extending hands full of gum.

We bought a few. Gum, not children. And with daylight we could see that the nothingness stretched to the horizon.

In San Quintin we found a street vendor serving tacos and bottled Coca-Cola, which was our breakfast. The taco man was friendly, and we called him Mike. Through a combination of hand signs and broken Spanish, I asked Mike if he could direct us to Shipwrecks. He smiled as one might smile at someone in a mental institution—and offered no directions.

San Quintin was a sleepy fishing village with simple block houses and low-slung tin roofs. It had the feel of a place either undiscovered or discovered and abandoned. The only paved road was potholed Federal Highway 1, and the land was slowly reclaiming the road. We found a store with mostly empty shelves. A thin layer of dust coated everything. We asked the shopkeeper about a shipwreck, and we left with bread, a jar of peanut butter, bottles of Coca-Cola, and a box of Tony *"el Tigre"* Frosted Flakes.

Since neither Mike nor the shopkeeper knew where we could find Shipwrecks, we decided to search every dirt road between there and Ensenada. After several dead ends we found a road that led to the beach. The road ended at a salt flat with a vast range of sand dunes beyond. I gunned the engine to cross the flats only to find it wasn't a salt flat. It was a mud bog covered by a thin layer of crusted dirt. We were sinking.

"Oh crap!" Erik had been hanging out the window, and his head was now covered with mud. "Don't stop!"

The truck fishtailed and sank and lifted and somehow made it across. We set out to cross range after range of dunes. We crawled the last few yards to the summit, wanting to surprise our friends. We didn't spot them, but we couldn't help staring at the infinite expanse of the Pacific. Sand dunes spread to the north and south as bold white outlines against the blue. To the east lay mountains, and the ocean to the west continued on to the curve of the earth and some distance beyond. But there was no wrecked ship. No friends.

Saying nothing, Erik and I turned to hike back. We'd have to cut a new road around the mudflats.

The next dirt road we found led to dunes that rose higher than the first. Reaching the summit, we saw a group of people and a boat in the distance. It wasn't a ship, but maybe that had been an exaggeration. The sun was at its peak, so we left shirts and shoes behind and hiked in the direction of our friends. We kept walking but they never got closer. Unrelenting heat bounced up at us from the baking sand. Everything shimmered. It was impossible to see through the glare, so we removed our shorts and fashioned them into hats and continued walking in our underwear. Still the distance didn't close. Our surprise grand entrance might well have us crawling in our underwear with sunburned backs and begging for water.

Finally we heard voices.

"*Hola,* gringos!"

It was a local family digging for clams.

Not to be deterred, we decided to try again farther to the north. We loaded a new tape in the stereo and found a beach-bound road. It felt different from the others. There were signs we couldn't read, but somehow they seemed unfriendly. We kept going until we got to a farm surrounded by green fields that reached to the sand dunes. We hiked another set of dunes and, from the ridgeline, looked for miles in every direction. No ship. No friends. As we drove back through the farm, the wind kicked up a memorable smell.

"What kind of plants are those?"

They looked familiar. We stopped to take a closer look and noticed a truck heading in our direction.

"Oh dude . . . we have to get out of here. Fast!"

We had stumbled onto a pot farm. Panic set in. Like everyone else, we had heard about drug dealers and Mexican jails. We sank down into the seats to minimize body target area and got out as fast as we could.

Once we had driven a safe distance, we stopped to make peanut-butter sandwiches.

✕

The search for our friends consumed us. Tension built. At the end of every unmarked road was a beautiful beach we didn't enjoy because it lacked friends and a wrecked ship. We searched partly out of obligation to our friends and partly because Erik and I weren't sure of our own friendship.

Most friendships are built on something tangible. Work or playing on the same soccer team or attending the same church. Those friendships tend to last as long as the circumstances that brought the friendships about. Switch schools or churches, and chances are you lose friends. Erik and I met playing in a rock band, and after years of practices and gigs and touring, the band was over. Men like their relationships to be practical. Shoulder to shoulder, not face to face. Though this works in the office, or in a band, it doesn't make for a meaningful friendship.

After another day of finding neither our friends nor a wrecked ship, we found a sandy cove and camped on the beach. Stars spread over a night horizon with the Big Dipper hanging so low it could have scooped water from the ocean. We were warmed by a driftwood bonfire, and our conversation went late into the night. We decided to give up trying to join someone else's adventure and yielded to our own.

We woke to perfect surf and spent the morning catching waves nobody knew existed. We rode every wave with our fingers intertwined with water. It was a subtle intimacy, like holding hands with the ocean. The day was freedom. Intangible. Impractical. Waves and peanut-butter sandwiches and bottled Coca-Cola and stories we never took time to tell.

We built a sandcastle. For an entire afternoon we dug and shaped, using nothing more than hands and tools fashioned from driftwood. Sometimes we talked while we worked. We talked of fathers and futures and girls who'd broken our hearts. Sometimes we worked silently. Completely free; completely ourselves. As we built the castle's defenses against the encroaching waves, we built our own defenses. The genuine acceptance of a friend will defend against any enemy.

The sun bowed to meet the water, its cape of colors spread over the horizon. We sat in fading light and watched the sandcastle fall gradually to the tide.

$$\times$$

There are places to which we never can return. Opportunities we'll never have again. The Northern Baja that we traveled in the early nineties is all but gone, the land now covered with condos. You have to take the dirt road when you can. Someday it will be a multilane highway.

Today Erik and I live in opposite corners of the country. Around our fortieth birthdays we made a point to get together. We talked about work and the challenges of raising kids. We talked about music and old friends. Then the conversation shifted and the light in our eyes shone younger. We talked about building sandcastles. Erik is the historian of our friendship, and over beers and laughs, he reminded me how we barely made it out of Mexico.

We had made one last stop for gas. After filling up I followed another car onto the highway and immediately met sounds of sirens and flashing lights. I pulled over. A *federale* approached our truck with hand on pistol as if arresting an international criminal.

"This *muy problema*," he said in border-town Spanglish.

"What's the problema? I drove just like everybody else was doing."

He stood at an angle that would ensure I saw his pistol. His mustache was full.

"*Problema grande.* You follow me jail."

"Jail?"

"*Sí.* Jail. Must pay ticket or go jail."

I thought through options.

"How much would it be to take care of the ticket here?"

The federale pulled out a notebook and pretended to study it. He was really studying us. We were covered in a week's worth of dust and looked like a photo that has lain in the sun too long.

"Forty *dólares.*"

"No *tengo* forty dólares."

"Thirty dólares."

Erik and I checked our wallets and together had little more than ten dollars. We offered it like wrists for handcuffs.

"Ten dollars?"

He looked at the money and then at us and then looked around the truck.

"*Sí.* And I take stereo."

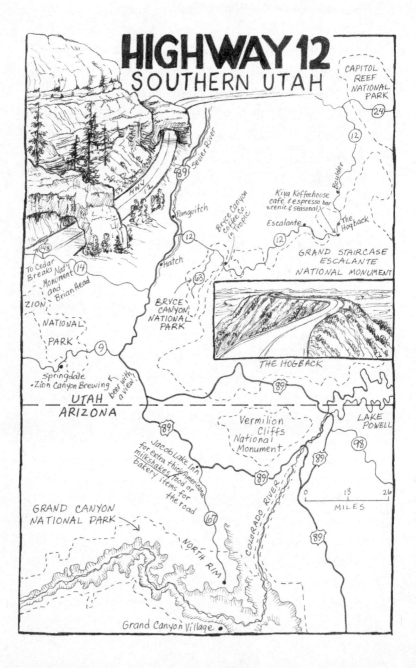

HIGHWAY 12
SOUTHERN UTAH

CAPITOL REEF NATIONAL PARK

(24)

(12)

Sevier River

(89)

Boulder

Kiva Koffeehouse
café & espresso bar
scenic & seasonal

The Hogback

Panguitch

Bryce Canyon coffee co. in Tropic

Escalante

(12)

(12)

GRAND STAIRCASE ESCALANTE NATIONAL MONUMENT

To Cedar Breaks Nat'l Monument and Brian Head

(148)

(14)

•Hatch

(63)

BRYCE CANYON NATIONAL PARK

ZION

NATIONAL

PARK

(9)

Springdale
•Zion Canyon Brewing

beer with a view

THE HOGBACK

— UTAH —
ARIZONA

(89)

(89)

Vermilion Cliffs National Monument

LAKE POWELL

(98)

Jacob Lake Inn for extra thick Americana milkshakes, food or bakery items for the road

(89)

(89)

COLORADO RIVER

0   13   26
MILES

GRAND CANYON NATIONAL PARK →

(67)

NORTH RIM

(89)

Grand Canyon Village •

4

Green-Dot Highways

Highway 12, Utah

There's a moment for every young man when the floor of the world drops from under him to reveal how big life really is. For me it happened on Utah's Highway 12 coming back from a trade show in Denver.

At age twenty-two, I had just launched a skateboard company with my best friend, Tim. My immediate job was to haul merchandise to the trade show in a rented trailer; then I had to head home so I could lead music at church on Sunday.

Before I headed to Denver with the merchandise, Tim and I reviewed trailer instructions one last time.

"You got this?"

"Totally. I'm good."

I'd never hooked up a trailer before. In fact, I'd never done anything mechanical that involved a car. This was a point of shame because I'd always associated being able to work on a car with becoming a man. Here I was faking knowing something about a car. Maybe I was faking both.

I got to Denver the night before the show opened and had to unhook the trailer so I could leave it in the underground structure. Unhitching wasn't bad, so the next morning I just reversed the order and got everything connected like Tim had shown me.

I headed through downtown Denver as buildings rose on both sides like canyon walls. It was morning. The sun hadn't yet reached the streets, which already were filled with sirens and honking and homeless people arguing loudly with themselves. I stopped at a light a couple of blocks from the 16th Street Mall to take in the scene, and that's when the car behind me started honking. I hit the gas and heard the ripping of metal followed by screeching followed by the feeling of being yanked backward. I checked my gauges, which were fine, then looked in the rearview mirror.

"Oh crap!"

The tongue of the trailer, previously connected to my trailer hitch, was wildly waving back and forth. The trailer was doing a wheelie through downtown Denver, only tenuously attached to my truck by two safety chains. I hit the brakes, and the trailer came flying, ready to jam the tongue through the back of my camper shell.

I stepped on the gas and ran a red light. The trailer fishtailed between lanes, then lurched forward lifting its rear in the air like a stinkbug. The metal tongue scraped the asphalt sending sparks up either side.

I slammed on the brakes and held my breath. The trailer tongue slid underneath my truck, and the full weight of the trailer smashed into the rear. The truck, with trailer smashed against it, screeched to a halt. The light was green. I put the truck into park and called Tim.

"Remind me again how to connect the trailer."

The trade show was a success. We made sales and opened accounts and discussed plans. We celebrated the unfolding of an unknown future and returned the trailer, and then I headed home.

I pulled over in Green River, Utah, at a truck stop that served open-faced turkey-and-mashed-potato sandwiches. The place had red vinyl booths and rotary-dial phones attached to the walls. The daily special was coffee and a shower.

I studied a map and found an interesting route that cut diagonally through the state on Highway 24 connecting to Highway 12. The line on the map had a lot of green dots, signifying it was a scenic route. There were other routes, but I had to pick one and that line looked good.

$$\times$$

After the first turn from Interstate 70, Highway 24 entered desolate lands of canyons and uprisings of earth. Boulders balanced on narrow precipices of sandstone. Ridges of vertical flutes like pipe organs reflected sunlight. In the distance, stones took on different shapes. Heads of boulders on shoulders of ridges. I imagined them as ancient giants protecting the land and passing secrets through the long void of canyons in between.

I made for the eastern entrance of Capitol Reef National Park, a hundred-mile spine of earth folded over on itself. In the middle of the park were remains of a historic farming settlement, Fruita, named for the orchards growing between the cliffs. The longest stretch of road lay ahead, so I grabbed provisions from a small country store and moved on.

From Capitol Reef, Highway 12 began a long, steep climb around the eastern front of Boulder Mountain. In a short time the road traversed several lives, each very different. Up from red-rock valleys and into stands of changing aspens with only a thin line between. Fall came early at this elevation, and I floated through seas of gold. The trees continued westward up the mountain until they outlined the sky. Beyond was a vista of cliffs and canyons and ridges with city-sized boulders that appeared as ants. I saw no end. There was only the beginning in which I stood.

The beauty was reckless. My mind tried to contain it, but it swallowed me. It was as if God created this expanse solely for His pleasure. From this height, the ridges and plateaus and spires and canyons and mountains and valleys and earthen folds looked like bright coral growing wildly on a tropical reef. It was an ocean of beauty; the highway my opening to swim out of shallow waters.

The highway dropped from the aspens along a serpentine ridge called the Hogback. On either side, the world disappeared. The ridge was nearly as narrow as the road, with the earth hundreds of feet below. The highway was all that remained.

I was heading back to lead music at church. The radio was playing music I would be playing on Sunday. I am not a lifelong church attendee, but since I've been attending, I've heard a lot about God's will. I know that it's perfect and gives God pleasure when I am in it. But there's not much clarity on exactly what it is. I've been left to believe that out of millions of options, I'd better pick the right one or suffer very hot consequences. It's a lot of pressure.

The problem is I've never known ahead of time what route to take and whether or not it was God's will. There are lots of highways. What if God's will was for me to drive through Nevada? Because of what I've learned from books and sermons, I think His will is focused on calling, or what you do for work. At first I wanted to be a rock star. Then I wanted to go into ministry. Then I wanted to go into business. Options were as endless as views from the highway. Finally I picked a path that included my best friend and had a lot of green dots—and sparks from a runaway trailer hitch.

After a full day of being on top of the world, I arrived in Zion National Park. I hiked into narrows and dragged fingers along red earth carved smooth by flood. I was waist deep in water, and the walls rose. Up and up and up where views along ridges will haunt the rest of my days. The slot canyon caught the late sun, and earth glowed crimson from within. I was deep in the grip of creation and could feel the pleasure of the Creator. I wondered if I would have felt it on another route.

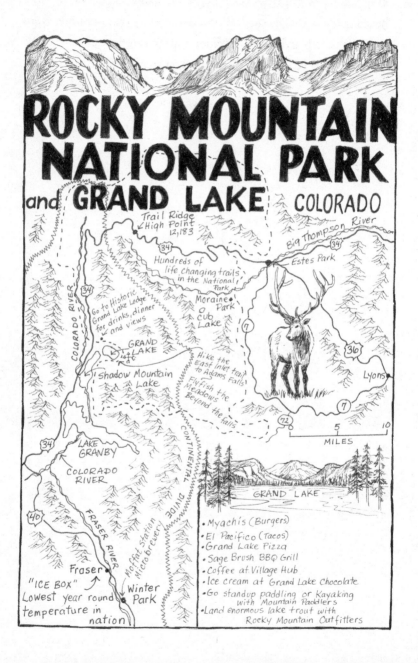

ROCKY MOUNTAIN
NATIONAL PARK
and GRAND LAKE COLORADO

Trail Ridge
High Point
12,183

Big Thompson River

34

34

Estes Park

Hundreds of
life changing trails
in the National
Park

COLORADO RIVER

34

Go to Historic
Grand Lake Lodge
for drinks, dinner
and views

Moraine
Park

Cub
Lake

GRAND
LAKE

7

Hike the
East Inlet trail
to Adams Falls

Shadow Mountain
Lake

Flyfish the
Meadows
Beyond the falls

36

Lyons

7

72

5   10
MILES

LAKE
GRANBY

COLORADO
RIVER

CONTINENTAL DIVIDE

34

GRAND LAKE

40

FRASER RIVER

Moffat Station
Micro brewery

- Myachi's (Burgers)
- El Pacifico (Tacos)
- Grand Lake Pizza
- Sage Brush BBQ Grill
- Coffee at Village Hub
- Ice cream at Grand Lake Chocolate
- Go standup paddling or Kayaking
   with Mountain Paddlers
- Land enormous lake trout with
   Rocky Mountain Outfitters

Fraser

"ICE BOX"
Lowest year round
temperature in
nation

Winter
Park

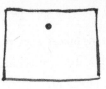

5

We Stood Upon Stars

Rocky Mountain National Park, Colorado

When it comes to backpacking, there is some debate about the appropriate way to wipe after doing as a bear does in the woods. During a wilderness course I took in college, a woman instructor insisted we had to pack out what we packed in.

"Everything?" one nervous student asked.

"Everything!" confirmed the instructor.

This of course included used toilet paper. To emphasize her point, the instructor displayed a plastic sandwich bag she planned to use. Her backpack didn't contain many compartments. She liked things simple. So this baggie would carry the souvenirs of her mountain stew next to her clothing and food. This was not in the brochure.

Fearful of starving in the woods, I'd eaten a couple of burritos en route. With the instructor's directive in mind, I had one pressing thought . . .

I'm going to need a bigger baggie.

A couple of miles into the hike, I was struggling to keep pace when I saw a male instructor hanging back, attaching several large-leafed weeds to his pack. He was really into nature.

"How's it going?" he asked.

"I think I'm developing a rash."

"Do you have any questions about the trip?"

"Yes. Are you using a baggie?"

"No."

This put me at ease until he added, "I'm using mule weed.

"Mule weed?"

He pointed over his shoulder to the leaves tied to his backpack.

"It's nature's Charmin. But be careful not to confuse it with poison oak."

"Um. Okay. Does it grow near where we'll be camping?"

"No."

"Then what do you use?"

"Sticks and stones."

I was happy never to go backpacking again until I met my new friend Greg. He was an avid backpacker who hadn't taken the same college courses I did. The first time he suggested we spend a weekend in the wilderness, I asked him, "Do you use a plastic bag?"

It turns out there's a toilet paper made specifically for backpacking. I asked the guy at the outdoor store how long this product had been on the market.

"This has been out forever. What else would people use?"

He placed it in my bag with my other purchases. Greg suggested we road-trip through the Rockies and backpack in Rocky Mountain National Park. The plan was to enter the high country through Estes Park and then hike a trail near the headwaters of the Big Thompson River until we reached Cub Lake. After the hike we'd continue along Trail Ridge Road, "the highway to the sky," driving above tree line and switchbacking at twelve thousand feet. Still new to backpacking, I didn't feel I was prepared for several days in the Rocky Mountain wilderness. But the day of our arrival was beautiful. Warm in the sun, but not hot, and cool in the shade. The air thins at altitude, removing anything of impure origin. My worries had no place.

✕

Cub Lake trailhead begins at the edge of an alpine meadow where headwaters of the Big Thompson River meander through the grasses and wildflowers of Moraine Park. Peaks surround the valley. Rocky Mountain National Park includes more than seventy peaks that rise above twelve thousand feet. They stand as pinnacles tickling the feet of heaven. These mountains are large enough to have a say in the weather, and they like to keep things unpredictable.

The first storm of the day found Greg and me on exposed tundra. It came from nowhere. One moment there was sun, and the next moment the sun was blocked by angry sky. The rain started first, descending in heavy sheets. Wind moved the rain sideways. Lightning flashed and struck the ground. I moved toward a lone tree and Greg yelled, "Don't get close to the tree! Crouch down in that low spot over there. Stay low on your heels." He ran from his safe spot to give me his tarp and show me where to stand. More lightning strikes. The world flashed with no delay between lightning and thunder. My body shook. At this altitude we were not below the storm; we were in it. I felt its power through my body. Granite peaks that moments earlier had seemed infinite now seemed insignificant. Lightning splits rock.

The earth and everything in it is subject to a greater force. I could see nothing but gray and water and wet earth. Lightning continued, striking as erratically as fear. Flashes stunned my eyes, like a light flipped on in a dark room. Then just as suddenly as it came, it disappeared. By the time I folded the tarp, the skies were blue.

Greg organized camp in a stand of lodgepole pines along Cub Lake. My bag was heavy and full, but it didn't contain anything useful. Extra underwear. Sketch pad. A couple of books. Greg carried the tent and pitched it in a flat area that was protected from the afternoon sun. He also carried the cookware. I helped him hang our food over a tree branch, far out from the tree's trunk to keep it beyond the reach of bears. This was a precaution to keep them from attacking our camp. My next job was to get water from the creek, but I had forgotten to bring a filter so I borrowed Greg's. I also forgot toilet paper.

With camp made we began dinner. Greg surprised me with a couple of steaks. His tradition was to have steak on the first night of backpacking. He froze it so it could thaw while we hiked the trail. Along with steaks were powdered mashed potatoes. We made a small fire and seasoned the steak with salt and pepper, smoke of fallen aspen, and the kindling of pine needles. We ate the meal as we watched a tired sun lower on distant peaks.

Cub Lake is known for wildlife viewing. If you remain quiet and hidden, you might see ducks and deer and elk, even moose and bears. Greg crawled toward shoreline boulders and signaled me where to go. Any time I made a noise, he pushed his open palm toward the ground, motioning me to stay quiet. All the miles of driving and hiking led to this opportunity to be part of the wild. Crawling in the dust tickled my nose, and I began to sneeze. Greg waved his palm so I stuffed it in.

The surface of the lake was covered with lily pads, and between wide green leaves, water reflected the pink of the sky. Ducks swam by the hundreds, calling each other in the twilight. Deer grazed along the shore. In stillness we had become part of the landscape.

My stomach began to rumble with high altitude gasses. Greg waved his palm. We found a place to sit on boulders behind lake reeds. Sitting upright created gravity for the gas. I tried to hold it in. There was movement on the far side of the lake. We could tell the animal was large, but it had yet to show itself. I was trying . . . Greg waved his palm . . . Nature came on strong . . . I let it go.

The boulder amplified the noise, and it sounded like the blast of a shotgun echoing between mountain walls. The once-peaceful scenery erupted. Ducks took flight, calling loudly to one another, trying to direct loved ones to safety. Deer ran for the hills and the lake surface boiled. After several minutes of chaos, the scene settled back to a calm state, absent any wildlife. Greg was quiet.

Finally I spoke. "Can I borrow some toilet paper?"

At camp we restoked the fire, settled in, and talked long into the night. Campfires are truth serum. I was dating someone at the time, and it was turning serious. I was freaked out because up to then I'd only opened up to a few people. This was a watershed moment as I decided to tell Greg about my growing feelings for someone who was important to me. He listened. He pushed me toward my heart, even if it meant less time for our Rocky Mountain road trips. Fire faded. In the glow of embers, we went to sleep.

"Hey, Rog. Wake up."

"What is it?"

"There's something out there. I think it's a bear."

We pulled out knives. Greg had a survival knife with a six-inch serrated blade and room inside the handle for emergency flint and fishing line. I had a Swiss Army Knife with a half-inch blade.

"What are you going to do with that?"

"I don't know. Maybe open a can of soup. It also has a toothpick."

"Maybe the bear can use that after he eats you."

There was scratching at the side of the tent, as well as snorting that was louder than our heavy breathing. Greg and I went still. I leaned in and whispered, "Dude, we're like a large burrito in this tent. What should we do?"

Greg was more excited than scared. I thought maybe we should play dead. I was about to share my plan with Greg when he shared his.

"Let's run out and see it. I'll go first."

"That's exactly what I was thinking."

With survival knife firmly gripped in his right hand, he grabbed the zipper of the tent with his left. I unfolded my Swiss Army blade. It was tough to get my thumbnail in the little crevice that opened it. I also unfolded the Phillips screwdriver from the other side. I still had twelve other uses and wondered if any of them would be helpful in fighting a bear. Before I could open other knife options, Greg was outside and I followed.

In the darkness we saw the creature. His eyes were black as night, full of nastiness. He saw us too and rose slowly on his hind feet, head moving back and forth with nose poked high to capture our scent. There was a shiver in the silence. At maximum height the creature stood little taller than our boots. We'd cornered a yellow-bellied marmot. It quickly realized it was no match for two grown men, armed and in their underwear. The marmot scurried into the bushes. Sissy.

Through a clearing in the trees, I noticed how close the heavens appeared. Among these peaks we stood upon stars. The Milky Way swirled about us and the earth went silver under the pale starlight. This world is so small in comparison to the heavens, and we are so much smaller than that. Small enough to be forever lost in the universe if it were not for the friends we travel with. Lowering my eyes back to earth, I saw Greg staring disappointedly at the bush that had covered the marmot's escape.

"It seemed bigger from the tent."

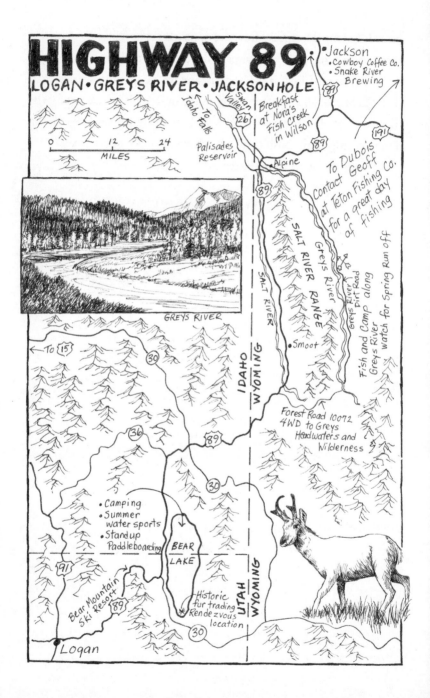

HIGHWAY 89
LOGAN • GREYS RIVER • JACKSON HOLE

Jackson
• Cowboy Coffee Co.
• Snake River Brewing

To Idaho Falls

Swan Valley 26

Breakfast at Nora's Fish Creek in Wilson

89

191

0   12   24
MILES

Palisades Reservoir

Alpine

89

To Dubois
Contact Geoff at Teton Fishing Co. for a great day of fishing

SALT RIVER

SALT RIVER RANGE

Greys River

Greys Dirt Road

Fish and Camp along Greys River watch for Spring run off

GREYS RIVER

To 15

30

IDAHO
WYOMING

• Smoot

36

89

Forest Road 10072
4WD to Greys Headwaters and Wilderness

30

• Camping
○ Summer water sports
• Standup Paddleboarding

BEAR LAKE

91

UTAH
WYOMING

Bear Mountain Ski Resort

89

Historic fur trading Rendezvous location

30

• Logan

6

Watch Me Grow

Greys River, Wyoming

At a coffee shop off Canyon Road in Logan, Utah, my wife returned to our ongoing conversation about having kids. We were five days into a month-long, cross-country road trip, and already the conversation had surfaced several times. Every time I had redirected it.

It was amazing how many things could make my wife think of babies.

She: "Oh, how cute! Look at that bump on that girl's belly. Know what that makes me think of?"

Me: "Uh . . . we need to get gym memberships?"

Five minutes later . . .

She: "Oh, how cute! Look at that "Baby on Board" sticker on that minivan. Know what that makes me think of?"

Me: "Uh . . . you want a minivan?"

Five minutes later . . .

She: "Oh, how cute! Look at that couple pushing a stroller. Know what that makes me think of?"

If I didn't come up with something quick, the next twenty-five hundred miles were going to be rough. I avoided the conversation because of fear, though I wouldn't admit it then. There is no map for marriage, so again I redirected.

Me: "Uh . . . want to get a puppy?"

The way my wife's eyes welled with tears made me think she was answering a different question than the one I had asked. However, we agreed a puppy was a good next step. We had the rest of the trip to discuss what kind of puppy we'd get. We also decided to name it Logan, after this town.

Logan is a pretty college town sitting on the western slope of the Bear River Mountains, in the northeast corner of Utah. We'd followed Highway 89 from the southernmost point of Utah, and this was our last stop before entering Wyoming. Fall had settled in the foothills with the soft gold of sun taking temporary residence in the trees.

We continued along the edge of the university, where students in backpacks rode bikes to class and all the women my wife's age pushed strollers. Past town, the winding highway rose countercurrent to a swift-moving trout stream. We traveled higher into the lush gold and green until we crested the summit and took in sweeping views of the turquoise water of twenty-mile-long Bear Lake.

We had been married less than a year when we set out on an uncharted road trip. For the most part, we would let the adventure come to us. The next fork in the road came shortly upon entering Wyoming. I'd read about a hundred-mile dirt road through a remote wilderness that roughly paralleled a pristine trout river. That was my choice. My wife's was the main highway, 89. She thought the highway would be a safer route, and I made a case for taking the dirt road. I asked her to trust me. She asked if I had our AAA card.

It doesn't take long in the wilderness to feel alone. It's when we're alone that personalities magnify and differences appear. My new wife wasn't comfortable with isolation. She liked street signs and the company of people. I preferred the company of trees. Trees act exactly as they should, and I feel safe in their indifference.

The farther we got from the main highway, the more my wife talked about snakes and chainsaw murderers and getting slowly eaten by a bear. All this I found more pleasurable than talking about babies. The dirt road climbed through a high pass and descended into a vast area of meadows and streams and pine trees. In every direction, peaks soared above eleven thousand feet. Sound was swallowed by wilderness, with thoughts and worries carried away in alpine winds. If they landed, they landed in peaks too distant to be a concern. My research said to drive roughly east on Forest Road 10072 until intersecting Forest Road 10138 to the north. There's a small wood sign signifying the beginning of the Greys River. "Watch me grow," it read.

At this point the river was barely a trickle. Every living thing, no matter how grand at the end, has the same humble beginning. An acorn. A fetus. A babbling brook. There's no idea of what will happen and no guarantee how things will go. There's only the hope. And a hope greater than fear is all we need to begin most adventures. I felt it there, listening to water whimper as pure as a newborn before filling its lungs. Headwaters are magical places. They live at the source of the magic and carry with it the hope of the beginning.

The brook grew into a stream that grew into a river. It gathered strength enough to carve a separation between two great mountain ranges. The Salt River Range to the west and a matching Wyoming Range to the east. From these peaks the river appeared as a thread stitching together a blanket of aspens and pines, yellow arrowleaf balsamroot and purple fireweed. The air too smelled of newness.

This trickle of water flowed about sixty miles until merging with the

Snake River. The Snake would merge with the Columbia River, which would merge with the Pacific Ocean, its blue swells ending on shores near my house. This water, like life, is connected. My wife and I followed the watershed, and it occurred to me that this trip was the headwaters of our marriage. It pointed to our own watershed. We would flow toward some unknown with nothing but a hope and the DNA of the beginning.

The river grew quickly. The land leveled into a high meadow, and the beauty was dangerous. It consumed me. We parked on the bank, and I entered the water more from instinct than will. My wife read while I set up my fly-fishing rod. I fastened a five-weight reel to a nine-foot rod and spooled plenty of line to thread the eyelets, leaving enough to make a first cast.

There was no fly hatch to indicate what trout were feeding on just then. But I'm most comfortable fishing with an Elk Hair Caddis and Pheasant Tail nymph dropper, so I began with that. My hands were numb with excitement, fingers clumsily attaching a thimble-sized fly to a hair-width clear tippet with six twists of a clinch knot. A fish jumped and my heart skipped and my hands failed and I had to tie the knot again.

The water's edge is a threshold. A first step into any river is an exit from one world and entry to another. Even though I was wearing chest-high waders, the water took my breath away. The river was wider than the road and flowed with purpose. It pressed cold and heavy against my legs. Walking required slow, deliberate steps. The river wanted to move me. Physically. Spiritually. Just as it had etched the mountains, it etched into my memory a portrait of a young man in love, both scared and hopeful of a changed world. All this—the hope and the fear—I felt in a tugged line and the rise of a trout. Light, heavy and patterned by broken clouds, entered the narrow valley like timbers holding back heaven.

The trout made a run. The drag engaged with the whir of line reversing from the reel. I reminded myself to breathe. The world stopped,

and I felt all the good that remained in the noble fight of a native trout.
The fish tired, and I gently stripped line through the space between my
forefinger and the rod. In the tension I felt the weight of glory.

I wet my hands and cradled the fish in light. The top of the fish was
colored as stone, a product of evolving defenses. The bottom the color of
undimmed beauty, magnified by pure light. It broadcast brightly with
pinkish red fading to a softer pink along the side. A native cutthroat. I
faced it upstream. As current pushed water through its gills, it gained
strength and swam away. A small part of me swam away with it and was
replaced by something better.

My plan worked perfectly. With every sighted stroller and baby
bump, we discussed what kind of dog we'd get. We decided on a golden
retriever. Changes would need to be made to the house. Gear would need
to be purchased. The more we talked about it, the more the changes felt
comfortable. Though I still couldn't foresee the outcome, our conversations began to sketch out a map of our marriage. It filled with topographical info. We built a travel plan to navigate the unknown, along with faith
and prayer and friends to grow old with. It was a map I could get comfortable with.

Upon returning home we found a breeder where the biggest puppy
of the litter picked us. He crawled clumsily into our laps and, with soft
breath against palms, fell asleep, never intending to leave. It was the beginning of something. The headwaters of love. Logan pressed with cold
nose and warm tongue against the first skin of morning, letting me know
before light there is love. I cradled him in my favorite chair where I sometimes read the paper and sometimes just had coffee. His fur was soft as
dawn as we warmed in the first sun through the window. It was hard to
imagine anything more perfect.

My wife walked in and said, "Oh, how cute. Know what this makes
me think of?"

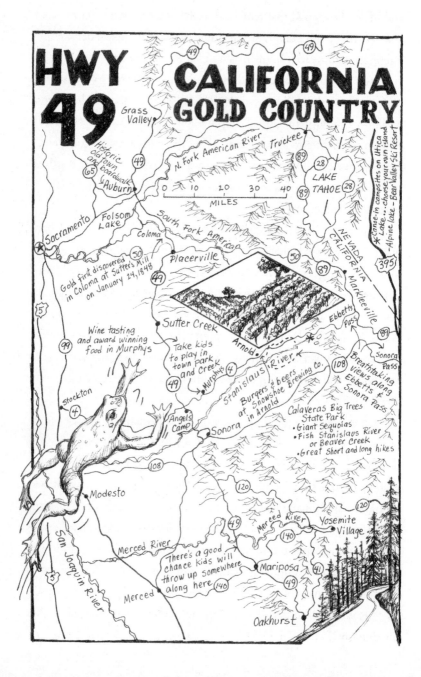

HWY 49

Grass Valley

CALIFORNIA GOLD COUNTRY

Historic old town and boardwalk, Auburn

65

49

N. Fork American River

Truckee

89 28

0 10 20 30 40
MILES

LAKE TAHOE

28

89

Sacramento

Folsom Lake

Coloma

South Fork American

89

NEVADA CALIFORNIA

395

*Canoe-in campsites on Utica Lake... choose your own island
-Alpine lake – Bear Valley Ski Resort

50

Placerville

Gold first discovered in Coloma at Sutter's Mill on January 24, 1848

49

50

89

Markleeville

89

Sutter Creek

Arnold

Ebbetts Pass

Wine tasting and award winning food in Murphys

99

Take kids to play in town park and Creek

49

Murphys 4

Stanislaus River

Burgers & beers at Snowshoe Brewing Co. in Arnold

108

Breathtaking views along Ebbetts & Sonora Pass

Sonora Pass

Stockton

4

Angels Camp

Sonora

Calaveras Big Trees State Park
•Giant Sequoias
•Fish Stanislaus River or Beaver Creek
•Great Short and long hikes

108

Modesto

120

San Joaquin River

5

49

Merced River

140

Yosemite Village

120

There's a good chance kids will throw up somewhere along here

Mariposa

49

41

Merced River

Merced

140

Oakhurst

7

The Old Ways

Highway 49, California

It's hard not to think about frogs when you're in Angels Camp. Everywhere there are plaques and photos and statues dedicated to the tailless amphibians. The town—as well as its frogs—was made famous by its frog-jumping contest and the story Mark Twain wrote on the subject.

In this settlement of authentic western storefronts, it's easy to imagine Twain spinning yarns in the saloon or writing them as he sat on the second-story veranda of the historic Angels Hotel. The town boasts a walk of fame for the most celebrated Calaveras jumping frogs, which my boys and I agreed was super awesome. My wife, at first a skeptic of frog monuments, eventually came around. Although she was glad to put the whole thing behind her and make a stop in Murphys, a beautiful foothills town known for locally produced wine, a vibrant art scene, and finely crafted food. I hoped for beer and fried frog legs.

We were en route to a mountain cabin for a week with our closest friends and the dozen or more children we'd collectively accumulated. It's an expensive hobby. I decided it would be fun to take my family the long way via the southern stretch of Highway 49, starting in Oakhurst and traveling through the boardwalk-lined gold-rush towns of Mariposa, Sonora, and Angels Camp. Though the map doesn't show it, from space you'd notice the middle section of the highway serpentines tightly in cursive lettering. It spells, "This is a bad idea." The ashen faces of my children only further reinforced my poor travel decision.

California's gold country first attracted attention in 1848, and in the years that followed, gold brought hundreds of thousands of people to this area. The forty-niners, as they would come to be known, staked claims along the middle section of the Sierra Nevada foothills, where gold was at first so abundant that loose nuggets could be picked up off the ground. This was rugged terrain, and for many years only the hardiest of souls could survive here. Many of the camps and gold towns are gone, but Highway 49 connects the remaining historic districts. The road follows switchbacks up the face of one mountain only to wind itself down another. In a short stretch the compass on my dash pointed in every possible direction, spinning like a pinwheel.

This was the only stretch of the highway I had not traveled before. I had fond memories of the southern stretch of the road, and I wanted to provide some good memories for my boys. Pulling up to the Hotel Jeffery in Coulterville, I realized my mistake.

"Daddy, why did you take us . . . ?" He couldn't finish the question because he had to throw up.

"You'll thank me for this experience later," I told the boys. But I knew they would never thank me, nor would my wife. She was busy comforting the boys while I studied the map, trying to figure out how to get us out of this mess. (They did thank me later. They thanked me when the experience stopped.)

✕

I first traveled Highway 49 on the back of Grandpa's motorcycle. The 49 was one of his favorite routes. It began near his mountain cabin at the southern entrance of Yosemite National Park, and the entire stretch corkscrewed its way north through forests and historic mining towns. It ended above the deep waters of Lake Tahoe. He always left the cabin predawn, layered in leathers and wool, and rode the first leg before morning shadows appeared. The curves of this highway had a power to unwind his mind. For any problem he faced in his business or life in general, the road provided a solution and a solace. Though he'd ridden the entire length more than once, it was the southern ribbon of the 49 he called home.

When I took my first rides with Grandpa, I was seated atop a decayed chair cushion duct-taped to the three-gallon gas tank of a 50 cc mini dirt bike. We explored back roads and dirt trails near the cabin, and when we weren't riding, I'd sit and stare at the bike like a dog stares at a tennis ball. As my legs grew longer, the motorcycles grew too, as did the distances we'd travel. Grandpa collected more bikes and parked them in ascending heights in the cabin's garage. The 50 cc. The Honda 125. The BMW 750. And finally, the dual sport BMW 1100 that had covered more mountain trails than I might ever see.

When we started riding the big bikes, my feet didn't reach the passenger pegs, so Grandpa rigged up places for me to put my feet and taught me to hold snuggly around his chest, grasping my hands together near his heart. I couldn't see the road from there and would wiggle in the passenger chair trying to peek around his shoulders. If I wiggled too much, he threatened to tie me with a rope to his body to keep me still. So I settled into long rides with my head buried in his back and imagined the views through changing scents of pines and wildflowers and old leather. I eventually grew enough to ride my own bike, but I never loved it as much as when my feet dangled freely and I held the heart of my grandfather.

The southern 49 became our ride. Grandpa kept a custom bag on top of the gas tank with a map visible. He folded it to show only the areas around the cabin, though he never needed it. And if I followed the map too closely, I wouldn't understand where we were headed because he had his own names for roads.

"Let's take the Old Highway and connect with the River Road and follow that into The Park."

This of course meant taking Highway 49 and connecting with Highway 140 in Mariposa, then following it along the Merced River until entering Yosemite National Park. I've traveled Highways 49 and 140 many times since, and they've never held as much wonder as the Old Highway and River Road.

I now travel with a GPS, but I'm still uncertain. We have at our disposal plenty of tools to tell us how to get places, but there are none that tell us where we should go. The road trip with the kids looked great on paper. I asked Grandpa about that section of Highway 49, and he said it was great on a motorcycle, but he'd never take a Suburban. I should have listened. We sometimes need more than a map to tell us how to travel.

My favorite River Road ride with Grandpa threaded the Wawona Tunnel, wound through the valley, and ended at the Ahwahnee Hotel in Yosemite, or as Grandpa called it, "The Old Hotel in The Park." We sat in wooden chairs outside the coffee shop and stared at the ancient granite walls of the valley. That's when Grandpa got to the big questions.

"When are you going to start a family?"

I'd been married for a while, and the question was a fair one.

"I'm not sure. I don't know how to do it."

"I thought you'd have figured that out by now," he laughed.

Before he offered to draw me some diagrams, I clarified my answer. I was scared. I was scared of a changing world. I was scared of how I would provide for a family and navigate the challenges of parenthood. I'd read the maps but didn't know what roads to take.

His demeanor changed. He leaned in and grabbed my arm. His hand felt warm against my skin.

"Listen, son. You'll be a good dad."

He went on to tell me things I was good at and the ways he was proud of me. We talked about the different paths a person could take in life. Grandpa had lost his son, my dad, to a dark road of drug addiction. Grandpa's eyes filled with tears. He told me there would come a time when I could no longer choose the roads my kids would follow. There would be heartache. Also, there would be joy. And the joy was worth it. When it came to parenting, he used words such as *hard work* and *sacrifice* and *prayer* and *trust in God*. Words that aren't used much anymore. They are followed even less. These are the old ways, mapped only by the furrows of faithful travelers. They are the only ways that can be traveled with any certainty.

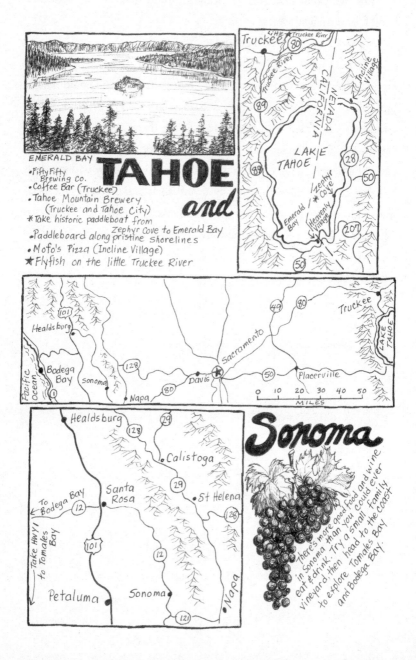

EMERALD BAY

TAHOE
and

- Fifty Fifty Brewing Co.
- Coffee Bar (Truckee)
- Tahoe Mountain Brewery (Truckee and Tahoe City)
* Take historic paddleboat from Zephyr Cove to Emerald Bay
- Paddleboard along pristine shorelines
- Mofo's Pizza (Incline Village)
★ Flyfish on the little Truckee River

LAKE Truckee River

Truckee

80

89 Truckee River

NEVADA

CALIFORNIA

Incline Village

LAKE TAHOE

28

89

50

Zephyr Cove

Emerald Bay

Heavenly Village

207

50

101

Healdsburg

49

80

Truckee

LAKE TAHOE

128

Sacramento

Pacific Ocean

Bodega Bay

Sonoma

1

80

Davis

50

Placerville

Napa

0 10 20 30 40 50

MILES

Healdsburg

128

29

Sonoma

Calistoga

Santa Rosa

29

St Helena

128

To Bodega Bay

12

101

12

Napa

Take Hwy 1 to Tomales Bay

Petaluma

Sonoma

121

There's more good food and wine in Sonoma than you could ever eat & drink. Try a small family vineyard, then head to the coast to explore Tomales Bay and Bodega Bay.

8

A Gathered Blue

Lake Tahoe to Sonoma, California

My wife came from a large family and was eager to begin her own. When she got pregnant, we prepared a room. We held a growing tummy and prayed for the life inside. We dreamed about his or her future and stocked up on bedding and supplies. We were headed to the doctor to find out the baby's gender and then to the paint store to pick colors for the room. Instead, we found no heartbeat.

My wife entered a grief I couldn't understand. Her body underwent a complete internal makeover. Mine never changed. She had felt a life, and it had transformed her view of the world and her sense of purpose in it. For me it was an abstract thought. A baby grows at the core of a woman's body. My wife loved this baby with everything she had. It's hard for me to love something I can't see. In marriage a wedge will grow in the midst of unshared grief.

We planned a birthday trip to Lake Tahoe. Its original intent was celebration, and I hoped the trip also could begin restoration. It was hard to leave our golden retriever, Logan, who had grown in size and dedication.

He visibly shared in our grief. With eyes of sadness and love, he watched as we pulled away.

We arrived at Lake Tahoe from the Nevada side, traveling west on Highway 50 after a long northward drive on Highway 395. From this quiet eastern entry, the lake announced itself without any preamble of roadside attractions or souvenir stands. Our first view was not of the lake but of a range of snow-covered mountains far to the west. The map showed the lake's width filling the space between two mountain ranges, the far mountains visible but at a great distance. My mind could not fathom the size of the lake. Then came the blue.

Along shallow edges of the lake, the blue of the water mixes with white sands and bleached rocks to deliver a Caribbean turquoise. Moving toward the middle, shades of blue deepen. It's not a different color, but a layering of blues until, in the deepest reaches of the lake, there is the purest experience of blue I've ever seen.

In winter the lake is outlined with a thick blanket of white, and in summer a band of green separates the lake from the snow-topped oval of mountain ranges surrounding it. Lake Tahoe is the largest alpine lake in the country and the second deepest. Outside the five Great Lakes, it holds more water by volume than any other lake in America. The water is gathered from snow and rain, creeks and springs.

We stood along the shore in morning stillness, our hearts having been twisted and dried of any remaining tears. Tears were replaced with anger. Storm clouds were coming. I thought God wanted this baby as much as we did. I thought God loved my wife as much as I did. This is what sold on Sundays. I looked to darkening sky and demanded answers, trying to comfort my wife after the loss of something I never knew.

At night the Milky Way reached with the long arm of God across the lake. I reached back but our hands never touched. Stars fell like tears, carrying their last memory of light. The morning came and water rose and the lake held. Grief is made smaller by emptying it into something bigger. It doesn't disappear; it only is made more manageable.

We went to a coffee shop in Tahoe City where my wife ordered tea. We took our drinks as we walked underneath pine trees, and sometimes we talked. I learned something new about my wife. I saw her strength and the depth of her love. Her strength and her love come from somewhere unseen, and I'm learning to trust in something I can't see.

None of this would have happened if we had followed recommendations of how to move on. This feels more like moving *through*. Tunneling through grief to some secret shore that we alone will share. We plant a flag together. Slow walks with hands held along the water is a bond for cracks in a marriage. And like the place where two broken pieces are joined by glue, the crack becomes the strongest point.

From Tahoe we drove west through the Central Valley, the heart of California, where anything good will grow. The valley is filled with small towns and farms and minor-league baseball. It is beautiful in the spring when the air is sensual and almond trees billow in pink and white. Traversing the valley is like driving through the produce section of our nation's grocery stores. Orchards upon orchards of apricots and nectarines, and miles of farms growing broccoli and tomatoes, basil and garlic. Food is ripe on the vine, waiting to be picked and shipped and prepared in kitchens across the country. This valley is the breadbasket of the United States, with more than one-fourth of the nation's food grown here. It often is overlooked because of California's glamorous coastal cities and Hollywood and mountain resorts. Also because it smells like cow poop.

The rest of our trip was spent walking the tamed earth of Sonoma County, staying in the historic town of Healdsburg, and visiting the area considered the birthplace of California winemaking. The earth was organized in undulating rows of vineyards. The vineyards were created with love, and the love could be tasted in every glass of wine. With a little distance we were able to talk about the loss. We walked vineyards, where we learned the best vines grow in struggled soil. We studied the vines, scarred with age. The signs left behind by years of pruning are easily visible. We also learned that the best wine grapes grow on vines with the most scars. Struggles and scars create richness and complexity, producing a wine worth sharing. Pruning is an act of love by the vinedresser.

Light enters this part of California in softer angles. It reflects along tops of vineyards where broad-leafed vines glow yellow green. Long rows distribute light over folds of earth, rising and falling slowly in quilted patterns of light and soft shadow. Every rise of the highway reveals a similar scene. Greens and yellows and golds are arranged in thoughtful symmetry, bordered by hazy silhouettes of low-lying hills and ancient oaks.

We drove along quiet farm roads where our grief was organized. Where do we go from here? What's next? At first I tried answering every question, thinking certainty was best. But the certainty felt dishonest. I didn't have answers, and any answers I did have were swimming in rosy waters of a shallow faith. More trials would come, and faith would deepen with them. When tended with love, the scars and struggles of marriage make for richer lives. Lives worth sharing.

NORTHERN
NEW MEXICO

84

0   11   22

64

Historic → TAOS
downtown & plaza

64

96

285

68

78

518

Taos Pueblo
World Heritage site
and one of
North America's
oldest continuously
occupied
villages.

84

518

Get lost in historic plazas
and narrow streets.
Then eat somewhere
that serves mole sauce.

285

599

★ SANTA FE
oldest capital city
in America

518

Las Vegas

OLDEST CHURCH IN AMERICA

San Miguel Chapel
in Santa Fe

25

50

25

285

41

ALBUQUERQUE

40

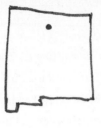

9

The Dancing Ground of the Sun

Santa Fe, New Mexico

The plazas of Santa Fe were cool in the morning. Everything lay in shadow, and dawn subdued the town with muted colors. Soon the sun would wake and colors would blaze. Red and purple flowers falling from oversized terra-cotta pots, bright chilies hanging from slats of faded pergolas, and galleries displaying paintings reflecting spectral colors of northern New Mexico light.

Until then there were only smells of bread and freshly roasted coffee. The scent drew me to a courtyard bakery where wheat-colored light escaped wooden French doors. I picked up chocolate-filled croissants for my wife and lattes with hints of cinnamon. At the hotel I was greeted by Logan, our hundred-pound golden retriever, who had taken my spot on the bed. He had managed to kick blankets over his body, and his head rested in the depression of my pillow. He didn't bother to get up. He rolled over and looked sleepily with tender brown eyes toward the bag I carried, as if to ask, "Did I order room service?"

Life had taken a dramatic turn. We had accepted an out-of-the-blue job offer in Nashville and were crossing the country with the few belongings of our young marriage. It was a road trip of shock. Every new view and smell was a reminder that we were headed away from home. We had tried to take time to talk about the change, but prepping for the move and saying good-bye to friends and family had dominated our days before leaving. So somewhere east of Flagstaff we decided to make a long stop in Santa Fe to talk about what was happening in our lives.

Santa Fe sits at the southern mouth of a broad valley where the high desert meets the southern tail of the Rocky Mountains. The light bends low. It touches the land gently, moving deliberately between wind and mountains. And though it is not seen, its presence is tangible. The light here always has been sacred. Earlier inhabitants referred to the area as the dancing ground of the sun. The area has drawn artists for a hundred years. It has drawn residents for thousands of years before that, including Native Americans living north of town in pueblos that remain unrivaled as North America's oldest continually occupied villages.

In a country as young as ours, any history comes as a novelty. Santa Fe is the oldest capital city in America, dating to the early 1600s. Its name means "holy faith" in the tongue of its founders. The history here is worn comfortably, like a favorite sweater. We walk below historic terraces and along battered walls. The sun is high. To escape the heat, we sneak into Cafe Pasqual's to order mole enchiladas made with Mexican chocolate and three different chilies. We then linger on plaza benches in the shade of elms. The afternoon light is fractured by clouds and dances along the Palace of the Governors, where locals sell their merchandise.

For as long as I could remember, I had made plans. They were carefully constructed around well-thought-through goals. Generally speaking, I would be rich and skinny. I'd read all the life-planning books and had filled out the worksheets and had prayed through my future and considered myself something of an expert on life plans. They were a great source of comfort, perhaps even pride.

None of the plans turned out as they were supposed to. The plans were a false courage. The books didn't work. I've since found that if you hold your plans tightly, you'll often miss the real call when it comes. The best of life usually happens outside your plans.

This was a hard lesson for me. I was unproven in the matter of change. I was succeeding in work and marriage, but I had a hometown advantage. My wife and I grew up in our little town, which was filled with family and friends, and we had a good dentist. None of this would be present in Nashville, but my wife's arms have the power to make any strange place feel like home. While on a walk I confided all this in a talk with Logan and asked how he felt about the change. He was fine. Logan was happy to be marking bushes in Santa Fe.

My wife asked if I knew the way. I didn't. Not really. There was only a small rumbling in my gut that said this was the right trail. In every man's life there's a moment of uncertainty. It usually comes at a crossroads of change. A man must act. Take a step. If not, he builds a house at the crossroads and watches everybody else travel by. We don't learn anything new about each other when nothing in our lives changes. When nothing new is learned, we get bored, though we might call it by some other name.

Santa Fe was a maze of history and regional foods and interesting adobe architecture. In construction and color, every wall seemed an extension of earth. The walls reached arm-like around buildings and parks. And sometimes, they reached for no reason at all. The entire town felt like an embrace, which came as great comfort for a time of transition. There's something about a town that has survived the uncertainty of ages that reminds us cracks in the walls only add to the charm.

Logan waited impatiently with our every stop to admire an arch or the way shadows fell against ancient walls. The only thing he was interested in was a bowl of water to refuel for the important business of letting other dogs know he was there. In this way he's like most men. The instinct was so strong that he would carve his name into a tree if he could. Lacking opposable thumbs, he went about the task in a more primitive manner. Not being able to hold a knife did not dampen his enthusiasm.

The day passed lazily in art galleries and leafy courtyards and by sneaking upon verandas, which usually led to kissing. Evening arrived with humility. Warmth, gathered through the day in earthen walls, radiated along side streets where we talked of change as we walked under soft streetlights. We came upon the Cathedral Basilica of St. Francis of Assisi, where for more than three hundred years, people have gathered to pray and hear from God. We stood in the dancing ground of the sun, sensing purpose in life's changes. Perhaps they were the plans all along, even if we hadn't recognized them sooner. We found a quiet courtyard and thanked God for speaking through art and light and adobe walls. Logan sniffed around and looked with his tender brown eyes. He honored the town in his own special way.

PHILIPSBURG

MONTANA

Missoula

Clyde Coffee

Strongwater Surf for river surfing, powder boarding and more

Blackfoot River

0   15   30
MILES

90

Drummond

141

12

93

Bitterroot River

SAPPHIRE MOUNTAINS

FLINT CREEK RANGE

Flint Creek

the Ranch at Rock Creek

Rock Creek

Spoon's Rock Creek Ranch

1

Clark Fork River

Skalkaho Falls

closed in winter

Hamilton

Philipsburg

DISCOVERY Ski Area and downhill mountain bikes

* Call Flint Creek Outfitters and Blackfoot River Outfitters for an expertly guided flyfishing trip.

38

Gem Mountain

GEORGETOWN LAKE

1

Anaconda

To Bozeman →

90

CONTINENTAL DIVIDE

THE PINTLERS Anaconda Range

43

MONTANA IDAHO

43

93

MONTANA IDAHO

Big Hole River

DOWNTOWN PHILIPSBURG

California St.

Philipsburg Brewing Co.

N. Sansome St.

Up N Smokin BBQ House

The Sweet Palace

N. Montgomery St.

U.S. Post Office

N. Broadway Street

Library

Gem Mining at Montana Gems

Flint Creek Outfitters

The Daily Grind

Doe Brothers Soda Fountain

Philipsburg Post Office

10

All the Wild That Remains

Philipsburg, Montana

Though there were no streetlights in town, lights flashed in my rear-view mirror. I saw them above the heads of my sons, who were eight and ten and excited about getting pulled over.

"Daddy, were you driving too fast?"

"Are you going to jail?"

As the officer made his way to the Suburban, I gave the kids some last-minute tips on what to do when you get pulled over. "Be sure to be respectful. No sudden movements. And keep your hands in plain sight. Any questions?"

"Will he use handcuffs?"

The officer smiled as he approached. It wasn't a sinister smile that indicated secret pleasure over busting another California speeder. He looked genuinely happy. We were in an area of restored mining-era buildings and towering mountains topped with snow and pines. It was easy to see how someone could be happy there.

"Where you headin'?"

"We've rented a cabin on Rock Creek but wanted to explore town first."

"What kind of boat's that?"

"It's a double kayak. Officer. Sir. But I can fit the whole family on it."

"You guys like fishin'?"

"Yes, sir."

"Take your boat to Georgetown Lake. Launch it in Rainbow Bay, and fish along the shores with a night crawler. Your boys will catch lots o' fish there. Don't forget your life jackets."

"Thank you, officer. Sir."

"Enjoy your stay in Philipsburg. Be sure to watch your speed."

As he walked to his car, I noticed the family we were traveling with parked across the street. Greg and Katie were laughing while their three boys' faces were plastered to the back windows, wondering if Uncle Rog would be thrown in jail.

Greg and I had explored the wilds of Montana more than twenty years earlier. We searched for big skies, big mountains, and space big enough to empty our souls of any remaining adolescence and replace it with the bigger hopes of manhood. On shores of remote lakes, we dreamed of families and careers and lives of romance and adventure. We threw stones into crystal-clear waters and asked for those dreams to come true. Montana delivered.

Since then we've married wonderful women, established careers, started families. The longings of single hearts have faded to be replaced with full lives. In this wilderness we dreamed boys' dreams and they came true. Now we have to find new ones. Fulfilled dreams of boys become millstones for men.

In addition to mountains we also sought meat. Not that California doesn't have meat. It's just hiding underneath some kale and served in restaurants filled with people in yoga pants passing judgment on meat plates carried by vegan waiters and served with a side of guilt. We were looking for unabashed, unashamed meat plates. Hamburgers, steak, buffalo, wild game. Maybe something recently hit by a car. So while our wives and kids discovered the thrills of sapphire mining at Gem Mountain and indulged in handmade candies at The Sweet Palace, Greg and I explored the places along Broadway Street, which made Philipsburg a finalist for the Prettiest Painted Places in America.

Within moments we discovered Philipsburg Brewing Company, which serves beers so amazing we wondered how it existed in such a small town. Then there's UpNSmokin BBQ House, decorated with statewide first-place barbecue trophies. The grill was parked in front and manned by a large bearded guy with a shirt that read, "Our Meat Is Hand Rubbed." He threw poppers (small paper-wrapped fireworks) on the ground in between his flipping of meat.

An open fire pit topped with meat will attract men from great distances, and sure enough a small crowd gathered. We stood in a circle and introduced ourselves with first names only, as if in a twelve-step program. While we got acquainted, kids started causing trouble in an empty lot across the street. The people in the circle got tense, as if someone in the town had relapsed into vegetarianism. As who knows what was going on across the street, the meat man pulled a slingshot from his rear pocket and fired poppers at the wall next to the kids.

Pop! Pop! Pop!

He rapid-fired poppers like a legion of archers. Kids ran and ducked for cover, and the meat man alternated between the grill and his slingshot. The circle of barbecue fans looked on with expressions of *Holy bacon!* Smells of gunpowder, plus hickory-smoked pulled pork and ribs, filled the air. When our stomachs could wait no longer, the tension broke, order was restored, and tables were set with award-winning barbecue sauces.

✕

On the road to Rock Creek, I wondered if the wild within me could be recovered. The thought was buried between doubts and second guesses about the trip itself. It was expensive, and I was taking a lot of time off from work. I've always had good reasons to not do things, but my boys were getting older. The opportunities would soon pass. If I wasn't careful, memories of things we did would be eclipsed by regrets of things we didn't.

As we drove I took in mountains and meadows and streams, and the old feelings returned. I leaned over the dashboard to watch a hawk soar in updrafts of summer wind. I craned my neck over bends in the highway to get a better view of winding rivers and wondered what trout swam in them. Unexplainable urges came upon me with every dirt road and distant peak. Hairs on the back of my neck tingled. Primal messages were sent through a straightening spine and landed upon restless feet. These feelings come back quickly because, for a man, they never really left. They just got buried under paperwork.

The mountains were as big as I remembered, and the only change was in the longings. I longed for life to be big again. For my boys to experience a father who climbed mountains and forded rivers and faced the wild in front of him. I feared my life was shrinking. We now have the whole world in our own hands, and we can access it at our leisure. We are shaped by what we commit ourselves to. We can look up and be shaped by mountains and sunsets. Or we can look down and be shaped by devices and yet another selfie. I longed for my boys to be shaped by all the wild that remains. I stood at the edge of the wilderness and looked up.

Our cabin sat on the Middle Fork of Rock Creek, at the edge of a working cattle ranch. The owner and her Australian shepherds greeted us and introduced us to the horses and calves we'd be sharing the ranch with. The rest of the herd was grazing farther up the mountains. Kristi shared stories of cows giving birth in forty-below-zero weather and the challenge of protecting them from wildfires and gray wolves. The ranch is isolated. When we asked her about raising kids on the ranch, she said the isolation forces dependence on one another. No matter what happened in their relationships, they had to come together to solve problems. Because of this, the members of her family share deep bonds with one another and with the land.

Views from the cabin deck extended for miles—first of water falling over boulders in shimmered light, then as a ribbon of trees and shrubs lining the creek. In the far distance rose peaks of the Pintler Mountains still covered with snow in late summer. No other structures or people could be seen.

The boys wanted to fish and to make a wilderness-survival video. Between the two traveling families, the boys ranged in age from three to ten, and even at those ages they were drawn by instinct to the wild. They forded the river and climbed a mountain and made a shelter. For the next several days, they explored water and woods. They caught their first fish on a fly. They saw a mysterious shadow that looked like a bear and went bravely to investigate. It was only the shadow of a tree, but in that shadow courage grew. They won't remember all their adventures. Experiences fade to memory and then the memories themselves fade. But with enough experiences such as this, the voice that called their young hearts won't be easily forgotten.

Twenty years following my first trip to Montana, I found the courage to chase new dreams. I dreamed of a life full of adventures with my boys and experiences that would shape the life of our family. I dreamed of how my career could provide the money needed to pay for more experiences together. A boy's dream is for himself. A man's dream is for others. It comes from the wild within, and the wild is ever expanding.

To recover the wild in us, we must first recognize our making. Every man has flames of wilderness ignited in him at birth. We are created from passion and bear the likeness of an untamed Creator. There is a voice of the wild, and as men we know it. When it calls we must go, in spite of the clamor of opposing voices that tell us not to. Our lives will be defined by what we choose. Along the banks of Rock Creek, I rediscovered a wild that never had been lost. I just had to return to the voice.

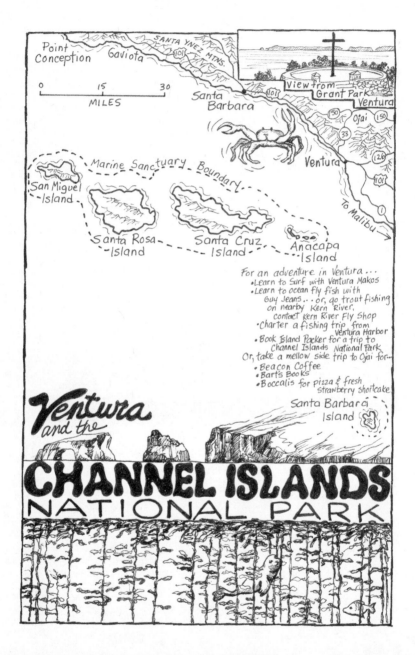

Point Conception Gaviota SANTA YNEZ MTNS. 101

0   15   30
MILES

Santa Barbara

View from Grant Park
Ventura

50 Ojai 150
33 126 101

Marine Sanctuary Boundary

San Miguel Island

Ventura

To Malibu

Santa Rosa Island   Santa Cruz Island   Anacapa Island

For an adventure in Ventura...
• Learn to Surf with Ventura Makos
• Learn to ocean fly fish with Guy Jeans...or, go trout fishing on nearby Kern River, contact Kern River Fly Shop
• Charter a fishing trip from Ventura Harbor
• Book Island Packer for a trip to Channel Islands National Park
Or, take a mellow side trip to Ojai for~
• Beacon Coffee
• Bart's Books
• Boccalis for pizza & fresh strawberry shortcake

Santa Barbara Island

Ventura and the

CHANNEL ISLANDS
NATIONAL PARK

11

Of Crabs and Men

*Ventura and the Channel Islands
National Park, California*

When people who don't live on the beach discover that I surf, they often ask if I'm afraid of sharks. The short answer is no, which surprises people. I assure them it's not because I'm superbrave. It's that my only shark sighting was in the Channel Islands National Park, while my brush with death in the surf was due to a much more nefarious sea creature.

For generations, C Street has been the home surf break for Ventura surfers. The waves form over a shallow cove between a short point of land and the pier. Since the ocean floor determines the shape of a wave, the waves of C Street break mellow and slow. On any given day, the lineup fills with beginner surfers and aging friends who have surfed every swell together for fifty years or more.

The break is named for California Street, a four-block boulevard connecting Pacific swells to historic City Hall and the independent stores and cafés of downtown Ventura. City Hall is perched on a hill overlooking the pier where hillside views connect downtown, the beaches, and Channel Islands National Park, only a short distance from Ventura's shoreline. Channel Islands is a protected sea sanctuary surrounding a primitive landscape of grasslands, creeks, and forests—and oceans as pristine as when Native Americans gathered food from the crystal-clear bays. Beyond the bays, the ocean's food chain swims in full abundance, with those near the top of the chain—dolphins, whales, otters, sharks— most visible. Lurking below is the creature related to my near demise.

On a recent day I came in after a mellow session with my older son. The tide was low, with the ocean floor covered by plate-sized boulders made slippery with sea moss. I've walked these waters for more than thirty years and am used to keeping my feet on boulders while leaning on my surfboard to offset my weight. I've never had a problem.

This time, however, it felt as if my little toe had been crushed between two boulders. The water was too deep to lift my foot above the surface so I could take a look. I assumed I had slipped off one rock and jammed my toe into another. With one hand on my board and the other waving wildly to keep my balance, I hopped on one foot to shallower water. The pain got worse with every hop.

My son, who heard me reacting to the pain, as could many of the people on the beach, came to help.

"What's wrong, Dad?"

"I don't know. I think I broke my toe."

The pain pulsed, traveled through my leg, and throbbed in some nerve center of my brain where I thought about what type of cast I'd need for a broken toe. To balance myself I placed both hands on my board and slowly lifted my leg to the side. When my foot rose from the water, a high-pitched shrieking followed it.

"What the . . . What is that!?!"

The screaming wasn't coming from my ten-year-old son or from the little girls watching us from the beach. It was coming from *me*. A forty-one-year-old man with a large crab attached to his little toe.

I kicked my leg and lost my balance and fell backward into the water. In all the commotion, the crab clamped on harder to my pinkie toe. I screamed for my son to help; he immediately ran as fast as he could away from the sea monster.

"That's okay, Son! Save yourself! Tell your mommy I love her!" Now I was alone in the ocean, fighting for my life.

I've spent most of my life on or near the water. It's more of who I am than where I went to school or where I work. I have great respect for the ocean. I've defined myself as a surfer, a product of a coastal town, and in younger years, a bit of a waterman. I took great pride in this definition. But on this day, the crab was challenging my identity.

$$\times$$

It's a little-known fact that crabs are the only creatures a great white shark is afraid of. That may not be true; I just made it up. But they should be afraid. It's easy for a shark to pick on other creatures because the shark sits atop the food chain. Meanwhile, crabs will attack anything, no matter its size. If I'd stepped on the crab, I would have crushed it. Instead, it was crushing me.

I regained my composure, no longer splashing like a child in the shallow end of the pool. I came up with a plan to avoid dying in three feet of water as a common shore crab consumed me piece by piece. Using my board for balance, I got back on one foot and raised the other from the water. The crab by this time was dangling casually from my toe by a single claw. It looked like a rock climber.

I wanted to stare into the eyes of my enemy, to see into its black soul and get inside its head. I couldn't find its eyes, but I noticed two little orbs dangling from the front of its shell. I moved my head for a better stare-down position. No luck. Each eye was dangling in a different direction, mostly to the side. The crab tightened its grip, causing my toe to give off signals that it was being severed from the rest of my foot.

I tried again to shake the crab from my foot, but it clamped harder. It tucked its eight arachnid legs close to its body while the non-toe-clenching claw waved freely like a cowboy riding a bull. I'd have to pry it off.

Then things got awkward.

I'm not superstretchy. It had been a while since I'd last touched my toes. My surfing was on a rapid decline while my weight was on a rapid rise. I thought if I held on to surfing I wouldn't feel so middle-aged. I'd become a version of myself I promised I never would—the nonstretchy version.

I wanted my sons to think they had the cool dad who surfed and did the things they liked to do. But on this day, their dad was screaming and rolling and splashing in three feet of water with a crab attached to his pinkie toe. I'd let us all down.

Survival begins with acceptance of current facts. I was getting older. Things that once came easy no longer would. I was no longer all that I used to be, but the best version of myself could still lie ahead.

Calming myself, I placed one hand palm down on the surfboard and gained sure footing with the noncrab foot. Then I bent my body, raising my leg toward my torso while reaching my free arm toward my foot. It looked like a yoga pose. It was the there's-a-freaking-crab-on-my-toe pose.

I got my hand close to the crab and realized how grotesque those things are. Its underbelly looked like a Batman costume with molded abs and slimy green goo between abdominal crevices. The top shell was smooth and rippled like a good skipping stone. Its claws were massively oversized for its body. Between its eyes, which still hadn't focused on anything, were two dangly antennae moving like garden worms. In the middle of all this was a mouth, constantly chomping, in anticipation of consuming my flesh.

With my free hand I tried to pry the claw open. It wouldn't let go. Blood oozed from my toe. I nearly fainted.

When it seemed there was no hope, that I'd be eaten by a common crab only fifteen feet from shore, I gave one last desperate kick. The crab came free. It skipped along the water a couple of times before sinking. The last thing I saw was a single claw waving defiantly above the water's surface.

I hobbled on my mangled, bloodied toe to the van, where my son was already dried off and dressed. He spoke first.

"We should have crab for dinner tonight."

PARADISE VALLEY
MONTANA

Country Bookshelf
(Montana's largest independent bookstore)

Yellowstone River

Bozeman

Museum of the Rockies
Lewis & Clark Caverns
(near Bozeman)   Livingston

90

Driftboat fish any section
of the Yellowstone River for
beautiful scenery and great
fishing

Conley's Boats
and Music

Pine Creek
Lodge and Restaurant

Great rafting throughout
the Yellowstone river — Book with
Local Guides

GALLATIN RANGE

Yellowstone River

ABSAROKA RANGE

Boulder River

Mill Creek Road

Mill Creek

Emigrant
The Old Saloon
& Livery Stable

Pray

Snowbank
Campground

Wildflower
Bakery

East River Road

Chico
Hot Springs

Saloon, Live music
and Swimming pools fed
by natural hot Springs
*The resort
is a fantastic
place to stay...
for a day
or for the weekend

89

0   10   20   30
           MILES

Tumbleweed Bookstore
and Cafe

Yellowstone Border

Gardiner

MONTANA
WYOMING

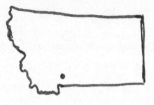

12

A Father's Fear

Paradise Valley, Montana

B e sure to get lunch for the kids."

The directions were straightforward. But Greg and I were on a quest in the town of Gardiner, on the edge of Yellowstone National Park. The wiser words of women faded into a muddle of manly distractions.

"What were we supposed to get?"

"Sunblock?"

As with any great quest there would necessarily be sacrifices.

Greg and I were searching for a section of the Yellowstone River safe enough for the youngest child in the group, around the age of three, to float down with the rest of us. Highway signs directed us to a rafting outfit, but other stops called for our conquering presence. Especially a place like this, which had a boardwalk for a porch, was clad in century-old wood, and looked like a shoot-out could erupt at any moment.

"Hey Rog, check these out!"

Greg was standing at a large crate filled with antlers. They were awesome. Also available in the store were rocks, used license plates, locally crafted beers, old maps, and unidentifiable rusted stuff. Not to mention a large supply of beef jerky. Just then an older woman with hair pulled back in a wild gray ponytail and in possession of a Montana-shaped body approached us. Clearly she was the shop owner, and one might reasonably conclude she won the shop in a hand of poker. Or a shoot-out. She may also have gone out to kill the previous owners of the antlers.

In a gravelly voice she exclaimed, "Them elk was horny!"

Our limited western vocabulary left us with no real response to this. Afraid of a graphic lesson on elk sex, I retreated to the beer and beef-jerky case. Greg, who is braver than me, later explained that elk shed their racks after mating season. The "sheds" are collected and sold in stores such as this with the proceeds going to wildlife preservation. He learned this while purchasing a nice rack.

Our education continued in the white-water-rafting store as we searched for a map of the river.

"We don't have any maps," said the college-age girl behind the counter. "But we have T-shirts with screen prints of the river on it. They're real detailed."

She slid a white T-shirt toward us. It had a crisply printed image of the river on it, complete with names of rapids and geographic features. It looked like a medium. She pointed to a section of river located below the left breast and said we'd find a stretch of water with only Class I and II rapids. Though because we were there at the time of lower late-season water levels, it might have a Class III hole lurking in there.

"So where does a Class III fit into the ranking? Is it like a one-to-ten thing?"

"It goes to five. And then, you drown."

It still wasn't registering, so we asked the rafting-place employee to hold her hand along her body at the height of a Class III rapid. In a beach town, all water-related danger is measured by the height of waves. Were Class III rapids waist high? Shoulder high? Double overhead? She was puzzled by the request, but eventually held her hand at a level that we saw as survivable. And besides, there would be life jackets.

Before departing for the river, we were asked if we needed a guide or a raft for the day. Both an officially licensed guide and a raft that was specially rated for these waters were available.

"Nope," we said. "We've come prepared with our own watercraft."

By "prepared" we meant an old canoe we found on Craigslist and a two-person sit-on-top kayak purchased at the acclaimed outdoor-sporting-goods store, Costco.

✕

I have built a safe life for my boys. I've monitored most of their moments, evaluating levels of risk and making sure kneepads were secured and shoes tied. I've rounded off the corners of coffee tables and have spied from windows to be sure the boys arrive safely at the neighbor's house two doors away. The real danger for my boys is that all the preventive steps make the world small. And a small world is not a good one for boys to grow in. I want them to see the world for what it is capable of being. Wild and wide open. An adventure to embark on.

Along the banks of the Yellowstone River, things are not safe. The river is unpredictable. Somewhere below the take-out is a place named Yankee Jim Canyon, a place we've been told our watercraft will not survive. We are surrounded by wilderness and wildlife. A snake longer than the youngest child in our group just swam among our young adventurers, who were wading along the riverbank. The snake lifted its head and, under duress of screams and shrieks, slithered into some vegetation. We are not in control.

The sun is high with unfiltered light warming thin air. Everybody is doing last-minute prep. The women are making lunches with food found in glove compartments and purses. The boys are securing life jackets as they look timidly over the water. Greg and I are tying his new antlers to the front of the canoe.

We were inspecting our work when the obvious question surfaced from our wives. *Is this safe?*

"We double knotted it. It should be fine."

Our wives looked at us, then the children, then back to us. We got the hint.

"Oh, the river. Yeah, totally safe."

We went on to explain how this stretch of water has only Class I and II rapids, with maybe a single Class III wave somewhere. Perhaps we should have bought the T-shirt as a visual aid.

"How big is a Class III wave?"

Greg held his hand at the height of his waist while I held mine at the height of my shoulder. He's not that much taller than I am. Bear in mind that our wives' request for food and supplies ended up garnering beef jerky, a six-pack of local beer, and an antler. So I'm not sure they were reassured by our respective gauging of Class III rapids.

To ease any concerns, we offered to give a quick course on water safety. We gathered the boys at the water's edge, next to the *unrated* canoe and kayak, and went over a few pointers.

"First, don't fall in."

"If you do fall in, get back in the boat."

"If you fall in and can't get back in the boat, float with your feet in front of you so you can push off a rock with your feet instead of slamming your head into it."

A couple of the boys were on the verge of tears. "Daddy, how big is the waves?"

There is some danger every father should protect his children from. Cars and bullies and lies whispered in darkness about not being smart or funny or good looking or talented. Certainly there are others, but these are a few that came to mind.

Still, some danger is required in a healthy passage from childhood into what comes after. Like falling off a kayak. If we don't let them fall, we can't teach the more important lesson of getting back on. One thing we can be sure of, though, they will fall.

LIVINGSTON & GARDINER MONTANA

"Where authors and anglers meet"

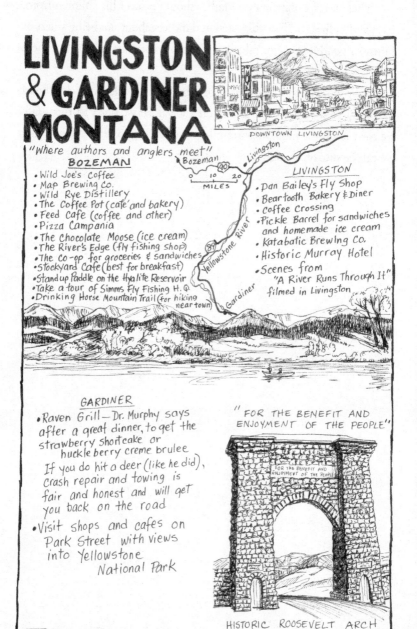

DOWNTOWN LIVINGSTON

BOZEMAN

- Wild Joe's Coffee
- Map Brewing Co.
- Wild Rye Distillery
- The Coffee Pot (cafe and bakery)
- Feed Cafe (coffee and other)
- Pizza Campania
- The Chocolate Moose (ice cream)
- The River's Edge (fly fishing shop)
- The Co-op for groceries & sandwiches
- Stockyard Cafe (best for breakfast)
- Stand up Paddle on the Hyalite Reservoir
- Take a tour of Simms Fly Fishing H.Q
- Drinking Horse Mountain Trail (for hiking near town)

LIVINGSTON

- Dan Bailey's Fly Shop
- Beartooth Bakery & Diner
- Coffee Crossing
- Pickle Barrel for sandwiches and homemade ice cream
- Katabatic Brewing Co.
- Historic Murray Hotel
- Scenes from "A River Runs Through It" filmed in Livingston

GARDINER

- Raven Grill — Dr. Murphy says after a great dinner, to get the strawberry shortcake or huckleberry creme brulee
  If you do hit a deer (like he did), crash repair and towing is fair and honest and will get you back on the road
- Visit shops and cafes on Park Street with views into Yellowstone National Park

"FOR THE BENEFIT AND ENJOYMENT OF THE PEOPLE"

FOR THE BENEFIT AND ENJOYMENT OF THE PEOPLE

HISTORIC ROOSEVELT ARCH

13

A Father's Courage

Yellowstone River, Montana

M y boys were nervous about putting the kayak in the river, partly because there were no seats for them. We put the younger in my lap, near the rear, and my older son up front on top of the bow. He was gripping a tie-cord that was attached to the nose for the primary use of carrying the kayak to the water.

Truthfully, I was afraid too. I was afraid they'd fall. I was afraid of being a horrible dad. I'm not a river guide or a wilderness-survival expert. In fact, I'm not an expert in anything. I struggle and worry and compare. I'm afraid of how I'll pay for this trip. I barely earn enough to keep our lives afloat, let alone this Costco kayak.

I look at snow on surrounding mountain peaks and feel water rushing past us as it has since the Earth was the same age as my boys. I exhale and think of who my boys are becoming and what this day will help them become. Even in my limitations, I know this is an important part of parenting. Before, I had convinced myself that my job was to protect my boys from danger. But that is not my job. My job is to curate their danger and help them grow from it. Life will be far more dangerous than getting through Class III rapids.

We put in at a gentle bend, where the water is wide and smooth and silent. To the east lay the Absaroka Mountain Range. It rises along boundaries of Yellowstone National Park and eventually, wild and unbroken, forms the tallest peaks in the region. The Absarokas contain some of the most remote wilderness in the country. The range is home to the largest natural predators of our continent, including grizzlies and gray wolves.

To the west is the Gallatin Range. Though slightly smaller in stature, the Gallatins are no less wild, with serrated peaks soaring above ten thousand feet. Cradled between these two great ranges is Paradise Valley.

We were carried through this paradise on the back of the Yellowstone River, which flows free and undammed for nearly seven hundred miles to its confluence with the great Missouri River and the gates Lewis and Clark first opened to explore the Northwest. We are here to discover something similar—not new lands but a part of ourselves made new by the land.

We get on the river, and at first there are no sounds but those of birds and the gentle lapping of water. As we settle into our watercraft the pace quickens, with sounds of lapping water turning into the steady cut of current. And we notice a change in the noise ahead. Or noises. Together they sound like an avalanche. I scan the banks and see there is no way out. The gentleness of the water belies its intention. We are sucked into a rapid, with no choice but to go through it.

A Class I rapid is defined as fast-moving water, and in no time we had navigated a Class I. This provided no reassurance. Each class of rapid builds upon itself, so a Class II rapid includes fast-moving water with churning on top and the presence of waves that are possible to avoid, if you know how to avoid them.

A Class III rapid presents a different type of problem. It includes intermediate and irregular waves that are unavoidable. It is not possible to go around them; going through them is the only option. Also worth noting, Class III rapids will swamp a canoe and can sweep a person off a sit-on-top kayak. We'd noticed that no one else on the river was attempting it in crafts such as we were using.

Greg's Craigslist canoe hit the rapids first. They turned out to be Class II rapids, but based on the water's surface, they appeared to be decidedly bigger than advertised. Next up, our Costco special glided through the rapids as elegantly as a barge in a bathtub. The kids hooted and hollered. Some new part of them came alive, replacing doubts and fears with pure joy. Fear can stunt and overwhelm joy, but when joy overcomes fear the sensation is multiplied.

Having conquered the first set of rapids, my boys have become a part of the water.

Ahead the river narrowed. As we got our first peek of placid waters beyond the next channel, it was clear the riverbed dropped from where we were. Other rafters had joined our flotilla. They, of course, had *licensed guides* and *rated* river rafts. As one passed us, I saw the guide seated on a bench. I gauged the height between the water's surface and his head to be about four feet, or "chest high" in surfer parlance.

We pulled into an eddy and watched rafters go wide-eyed through the channel just before they disappeared entirely. All we heard were screams, followed by silence. Then cheers as we saw them celebrate their survival farther down. Other rafts had by now piled behind us, so it was time for the Craigslist canoe and Costco kayak to prove themselves.

We went through the rapids first, but not because we wanted to. I had no control over the kayak. We spun in circles, and I hoped we wouldn't hit the fastest currents sideways. The great irony of the river is the calm before the terror. As we hit the calm we could see what awaited us below.

At random intervals across the channel, large tooth-like boulders jutted ominously above the foaming white of angry water. It looked more like a rabid dog than a river. And though there was sound, any distinctions in character had disappeared. Every sound in the known universe had been sucked into the river and whipped and tossed and amplified until it felt like we were screaming into a jet engine at takeoff.

My older son, who sat on the bow of the kayak with nothing but the tie-cord to hold, was momentarily suspended in the air, legs kicking at nothingness as the nose poked beyond the first drop. We went as a family, taking the first wave dead on, plunging through its jowls and out the back completely soaked but intact. We were hit immediately by the next wave somewhat from the side, threatening to spin us into the following rapid sideways. I jammed my paddle in the water and somehow, miraculously kept us straight. Though later I would take full credit for it.

Next came a series of whoop-de-dos. They lacked organization and sent our kayak in multiple directions at once. The front of the kayak was on a different plane from the back, as if one tectonic plate had risen above the next. I could hear faint screaming from my son only a few feet in front of me.

A few days earlier we had purchased a cowboy hat for him, and sure enough he looked like a bull rider with nothing but a cord to prevent him from launching into the atmosphere. On the next wave he was launched. His four-foot-three-inch frame was sent at a forty-five-degree angle directly off the side. With one hand tethered by the cord, his feet continued higher than his head before he landed into the last wave.

He disappeared for a moment with only his cowboy hat and arm visible above water. In a single urgent movement, he one-armed his way back onto the bow, laughing at the top of his lungs.

As we reached the calm water beyond the rapids, we turned to see how our companions would fare, expecting the worst. Greg's passenger-seating system was to have his wife in the front of the canoe, putting her in danger first. One might question the wisdom of that. In between adults, their oldest boy sat near the rear by Greg, and his two youngest sat in the bottom of the canoe in the middle, white knuckles gripped tightly to the gunwales and heads barely showing above the side profile of the canoe. Had there been parents from California watching us, calls would have been made to Child Protective Services.

They paddled into the raging water, and the canoe tracked gracefully through sections of Class I's and II's. They hit every wave perfectly. Other rafters gathered to watch and were amazed, then nervous as Greg and his crew got into position for the last wave, a solid Class III. Just as his wife was taking the brunt of the wave, Greg did two ferocious back paddles, which raised the front of the canoe only slightly but enough to go a little over, instead of under, the wave. Still the wave was large enough that they disappeared for a heart-stopping moment.

Those of us below positioned ourselves to prepare to retrieve kids from the river. They then reappeared from the Class III with hoots and hollers echoing along riverbanks. There was spontaneous applause. The kids in the canoe beamed with pride. However, the adults still paddled furiously toward the bank. I wasn't sure why at first, but then I realized the canoe was sitting lower in the water. We followed them toward the bank as the canoe took on water and settled onto a gravel bar. The kids swam to shore to meet my boys.

"Did you see us do a submarine in that wave?"

"Yeah! Did you see me fly off the kayak?"

"That was awesome!"

"Those waves were so big!"

"Can we go again, Dad?"

"Again! Again!"

The kids shared stories of conquest. In each retelling the waves got bigger, the snakes got longer, and the boys stood taller. Since before rivers had names, they carried the spirit of the One who divided the waters. Water begins in the high reaches and purer places. Within the banks of the Yellowstone it has power to make us new. As the boys talked about rivers and mountains, there was a noticeable swagger in their voices. There was something different about them. They were no longer afraid, and perhaps neither was I.

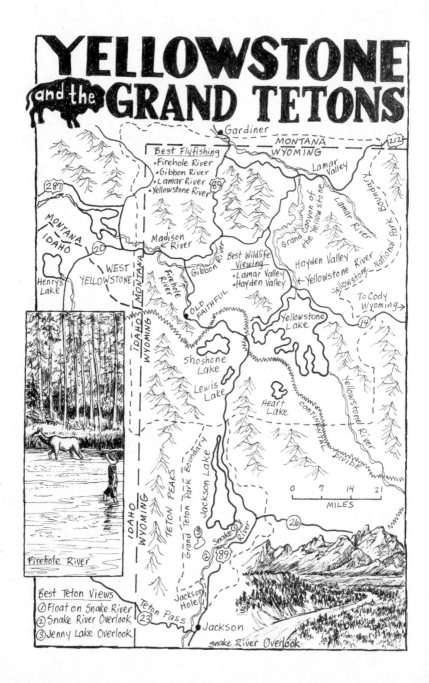

YELLOWSTONE
and the GRAND TETONS

Gardiner

MONTANA
WYOMING

212

Best Flyfishing
• Firehole River
• Gibbon River
• Lamar River
• Yellowstone River

Lamar Valley

287

89

Lamar River

Yellowstone National Park Boundary

MONTANA
IDAHO

20

WEST
YELLOWSTONE

Madison
River

Gibbon River

Best Wildlife
Viewing
• Lamar Valley
• Hayden Valley

Grand Canyon of the Yellowstone

Hayden Valley

Yellowstone River

Henry's
Lake

Firehole
River

OLD
FAITHFUL

To Cody
Wyoming →

14

MONTANA

IDAHO
WYOMING

Yellowstone
Lake

Shoshone
Lake

Lewis
Lake

Heart
Lake

CONTINENTAL DIVIDE

Yellowstone River

0   7   14   21
MILES

Firehole River

Jackson Lake

Teton Peaks

Grand Teton Park Boundary

IDAHO
WYOMING

Snake River

26

3

2 89

Jackson
Hole

Best Teton Views
① Float on Snake River
② Snake River Overlook
③ Jenny Lake Overlook

Teton Pass

23

Jackson

Snake River Overlook

14

Altars of the Wild

Yellowstone National Park, Wyoming

Summer arrived, another milestone marking the uncomfortable passage of time. As a father I've come to realize summers are few and—if I'm not careful—will slip through the cracks as nothing more than a season of hauling kids from activity to activity.

But summers offer a bigger opportunity. A chance for adventure to shape souls of young boys who, in a not-too-distant summer, will become men. All boys are shaped by something—neighborhood kids, video games, teachers, coaches—with results that reflect that which did the shaping. Though it's a disappearing art in our culture, the true shaping of boys is the province of fathers. One of the greatest tools for this task is the relentless wonder of this world and the deeper magic behind it.

This summer I've called upon the peaks and cauldrons and wide-meadowed valleys of Yellowstone National Park to partner in the effort. We arrived here along the same path as fire. In 1988 a wildfire closed the park, and decades later the land was still recovering. But in scars of death new life grew, as if death had never come here at all. It was deep magic.

I was about the age of my boys when my grandpa first brought me to Yellowstone. He believed seeing places such as this would expand my imagination and open my world. Grandpa wanted to know how things worked, and he took time to figure them out. There were very few times I asked Grandpa a question that he didn't have an answer.

Once, in the middle of our Yellowstone trip, we took a daylong detour to the Buffalo Bill museum in Cody, Wyoming, just so he could learn more about cowboys. He reminded me of a cowboy. He was larger than life as he explained how geysers result from steam pressure that builds up from boiling water underground. When the road clogged with bison, Grandpa said he was herding them, only deepening my belief that he was in reality a cowboy. Since that trip with my grandpa, I have thought often of the wilds of Yellowstone. Now that I'm a father, I wanted to bring my boys here to experience the same.

There's a Grand Loop Road through Yellowstone that bisects Hayden Valley, where bison roam by the thousands. They lounge along fields above the Yellowstone River, eating green grasses that in summer fade to gold. In the distance they appear small against the landscape. The valley branches between low hills timbered with patches of pine along the ridges. Beyond, in every direction, is a rim of mountain peaks.

Up close the bison are large, nearly the size of a small car. They also are clearly in charge of traffic, blocking roads seemingly for the pleasure of having their pictures taken. Our Suburban was surrounded. A stubborn bison blocked our vehicle and wouldn't budge, so I inched toward it.

"Dad! What are you doing?"

"I'm herding wild bison."

"That's awesome!"

My wife wasn't as excited about bison herding. As I inched closer, the bison's head rose above the hood of our SUV. They look really big up close. From another bison standing alongside the vehicle came a sound that requires no interpretation and results in immediate hysterics in any boy under the age of twelve.

Brother 1: "Dad, I just heard that buffalo fart!"

Dad (looking to turn this into a learning opportunity): "It's actually not a buffalo, it's a North American bison. Buffalo live in Africa and Asia. And that wasn't a fart, it was a burp."

Brother 2: "That was so awesome!"

Brother 1: "Mom, did you hear that burp? It was so loud!"

Mom: "Yes, I heard it." And then, trying to change the subject, "Look at those baby bison."

Brother 1: "Oh my gosh, it was so loud. I want to burp that loud."

Brother 2: "I bet you can't."

Brother 1: "Dad, do we have any soda?"

Mom: "That's enough. I've heard enough about burping. Let's talk about something else."

This worked for a moment until another bison broke the silence.

Dad: "If that was a fart, it could have started a forest fire."

Hysterics in the backseat.

Smack. It came from the passenger side of the front seat.

Dad: "Ouch!"

Toward the end of the loop, we stopped at Old Faithful. The boys grew restless, no longer interested in tame environments of visitor centers or boardwalks crowded with other onlookers.

"Dad, how long is this going to take? I'm bored."

I tried to teach them some things about geysers—the things they missed in the visitor center because they were busy fighting with each other. I told them geysers are created by steam escaping from deep in the earth. I explained that Old Faithful was one of the most predictable natural features on earth, erupting every ninety minutes.

"That's soooo long."

Just then water started to bubble and sputter, and from the depths of the earth erupted eight thousand gallons of boiling water that shot well above one hundred feet into the sky. The geyser's noise and its towering plume of steam shocked my boys into silence. There is no way to explain a phenomenon such as this. It has to be experienced, like fireworks and ice cream on July Fourth. The concussive thunder that rattles your ribcage. The hiss of water returning to earth after a long journey to the sky. This is a memory that will stick. Thirty years later it still sticks with me when I think back to first seeing it with my grandfather. In a chaotic world it's comforting to still be able to rely on some things. Like Old Faithful. Like Grandpa.

These things are governed by something bigger than this world. Deep magic.

We made camp at Madison Junction, where the Gibbon and Firehole Rivers merge to create the Madison River. A large Y-shaped funnel with a meadow in the middle lies at the intersection of the three rivers. The meadow backs to a dark forest. Above the merge there's a lazy bend of the Gibbon running shallow and slow along a sandbar. It's a great place for families to picnic and kids to swim. On the far side of the river, the meadow appears as an island between the rivers and the woods. It looked full of adventure and unknown treasures. It also looked full of danger. I know what lives in dark woods, and I'd rather leave them alone. As the kids swam we kept an eye on the island and the dark forest beyond.

My older son decided to go upstream, just out of earshot, and crossed to explore the island. It made me nervous. He crossed the river the way we had practiced, taking a slow, wide stance and keeping the thinnest part of his body against the current. On the far side, grasses ran wilder and taller.

He first explored around the bank, then moved in toward the woods. His head dipped below the grass and I held my breath, as if he were underwater. I saw his head again and exhaled, relieved. Then I saw something else. The grass beyond my son was moving. I started toward the river crossing.

I couldn't see what was in the grass, but as I closed in I could tell it was large. My son saw me moving quickly toward him and then heard the movement. What looked like large dead branches rose high above the grass. They were attached to the head of a bull elk that stood twice as tall as my son. Behind the huge elk was a herd. The elk sniffed for signs of danger. A bull elk will do anything to protect his herd.

The river separated my son from me and nothing separated him from the elk. There was no way I could get to my son before the elk did. I prayed he wouldn't run or yell or do anything to spook it. Again he did exactly what we talked about. He kept his eyes fixed on the elk and crossed back over the river. He moved slowly, waist deep in the current. Another elk entered the river only a few yards beyond. There was a moment when both my son and the elk were midriver, eyes locked on each other, surrounded by the grandeur of mountains and meadows and forests.

A time comes when we look up to see that the world is bigger than we thought. It is filled with wonder and deeper magic. We know the moment when the world pauses and time stands still. When the entire glory of the universe is focused on communicating something bigger than our limited language allows, so we receive it through tingling hairs on the backs of our necks. My son received it along the banks of the Gibbon and Firehole while being sized up by a wild animal several times his size.

When my son crossed back to the near side of the river he sprinted into my arms. His heart was racing. He said he wasn't scared because he knew what to do. Something had happened within him. A back door to curiosity opened, and he listed new questions. We sat along the riverbank and discussed them all. I didn't have some of the answers he needed. However, by sitting in the cauldron of Yellowstone, we received answers even for questions we didn't know how to ask.

Throughout history a place was considered sacred when someone encountered the deep magic there. In all cases the people were moved to action. Some prayed. Some gave thanks. Some erected altars of stacked stone. Sacred places still exist. They are found in mountains and deserts and along oceans, and we're drawn to them, sometimes unexplainably. As the sun dips, casting its last untamed light, the world goes aglow in colors that artists have attempted to re-create since the invention of the paint-brush. Here we cry out.

"If there's someone out there, will you . . ."

"God, please help."

"This is freakin' awesome!"

"Thanks."

We give our time and worries and hopes, and in exchange, we receive assurances. They're spoken in a voice with no tongue that is understood by all peoples of all time. It's the light of the canyon. The wind through broad-leafed hardwoods. It's the voice of something bigger at work in this world, and like a child sitting in the lap of a father, we feel safe in our smallness. We erect altars in the wild to give thanks for the deep magic that meets us there.

As my boys grow I hope they'll occasionally think of Yellowstone and bison and Old Faithful. When they do, I hope they'll be reminded of a father who loved them and tried to teach something of this world, even if it seemed boring at the time. And I hope someday they will take their own kids to sacred places and experience the deep magic. I hope, in response, that they will erect their own altars there.

Leaving the park, I wanted to see how much everybody had learned. A lot gets invested into summer travel, and the hope is that something important will stick with everybody. Maybe something that shifts the way we think about the world, forever altering the path we travel. Places as magical as Yellowstone have the power to do this.

Dad: "Hey, everyone. I have an important question about our trip. What did you guys learn about Yellowstone?"

Brother 1: "Yellowstone is awesome! I saw a moose."

Dad: "Did you learn anything cool about moose?"

Brother 2: "I learned that they have really big poop."

Brother 1: "That's awesome! Did you see any bear poop? I bet it's huge!"

My wife could see where this was headed. She tried to rescue the conversation.

Mom: "I learned that Old Faithful goes off every ninety minutes."

Dad: "See, guys? That's pretty interesting, right? Is there anything else you learned?"

Brother 2: "I learned that a buffalo is really a bison."

Dad: "That's great!"

Brother 2: "And their farts can start a forest fire."

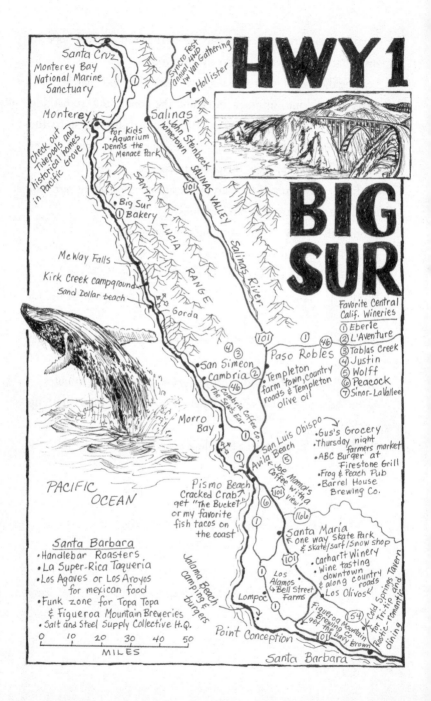

HWY 1

Santa Cruz
Monterey Bay National Marine Sanctuary

Syncro Fest Annual 4WD VW Van Gathering
Hollister

Monterey

Salinas — John Steinbeck hometown

Check out Tidepools and historical homes in Pacific grove

For kids
• Aquarium
• Dennis the Menace Park

SANTA LUCIA RANGE

SALINAS VALLEY

Salinas River

101

• Big Sur
① Bakery

BIG SUR

McWay Falls
Kirk Creek campground
Sand Dollar beach

Gorda

Favorite Central Calif. Wineries
① Eberle
② L'Aventure
③ Tablas Creek
④ Justin
⑤ Wolff
⑥ Peacock
⑦ Sinor-LaVallee

101   ① 46
Paso Robles

④ ③
• San Simeon
Cambria ②

The Sow's Ear
Cambria Coffee Co.

• Templeton farm town, country roads & Templeton olive oil

Morro Bay

San Luis Obispo

① Avila Beach
⑦   ⑤

Joe Momo's Coffee with a view!

• Gus's Grocery
• Thursday night farmers market
• ABC Burger at Firestone Grill
• Frog & Peach Pub
• Barrel House Brewing Co.

PACIFIC OCEAN

Pismo Beach
Cracked Crab—get "The Bucket" or my favorite fish tacos on the coast

101
⑥
①

① 166

Santa Maria
one way Skate Park & skate/surf/snow shop

Santa Barbara
• Handlebar Roasters
• La Super-Rica Taqueria
• Los Agaves or Los Aroyos for mexican food
• Funk zone for Topa Topa & Figueroa Mountain Breweries
• Salt and Steel Supply Collective H.Q.

Jaloma Beach camping & burgers

101
①

Los Alamos
Bell Street Farms

Lompoc

• Carhartt Winery
• Wine tasting downtown & along country roads
Los Olivos

Figueroa Mountain Brewing Co.
Get the Davy Brown

54
Cold Springs Tavern for Tri-tip and Rustic-romantic dining

①
101

Point Conception

Santa Barbara

0 10 20 30 40 50
MILES

15

Highway Poetry

Highway 1, Santa Barbara to Big Sur, California

As a young man, I thought a lot about vans. I came by it honestly, living for a time as a child in a Santa Cruz hippie commune. Shortly after, my dad and uncle built a tiny home on the back of a partially restored 1939 two-and-a-half-ton flatbed Dodge. The home was complete with a rock fireplace, secondhand stove, and paisley window curtains sewn by my mom. I have cherished photos of living there for a time on new beach property created by the carving of a freeway north of Ventura, California. Since the land was new, my uncle was able to homestead the property and was eventually dubbed the "mayor of oil piers." I look at the photos often, though they are fading along with the freedom of that age.

When I turned sixteen, my natural inclination was to purchase a VW van, paint it myself, and spend the summer exploring back roads of America. As awesome as this sounded, the road-trip scenario was vastly improved by the thought that the girl I loved at the time would accompany me. She'd sit in the passenger seat with her blond hair tussled by desert winds whistling through rolled-down windows over the music of "Fields of Gold" by Sting. She and I talked once about taking the trip, but when my birthday rolled around, I was given a decade-old, two-seater Toyota truck, and our conversations drifted toward how our relationship would be better as friends.

I lost the girl but not the dream. It was eventually replaced with an even better reality. My honeymoon brought the next opportunity for a cross-country road trip with a beautiful girl. My wife and I traveled Highway 1 north along the central California coast, between Santa Barbara and Carmel. Everything was exciting and new, and sex came intense and fast. We stayed in affordable hotels and camped out in the back of my truck. But it wasn't a van, and it wasn't until years later that I had the chance to realize my dream. Our ten-year anniversary present to each other was a VW Westfalia Syncro purchased through the Internet from its owner, who lived in Bozeman, Montana. We named the van Madison, after a favorite fly-fishing river nearby, and once the van arrived at our home, we made plans to retrace our honeymoon trip.

VW vans loom large in American road-tripping mythology. Like horses in a previous time, they symbolize freedom. VW vans possess other similarities to horses. They are exactly one horsepower, for instance. Any hill requires shifting down into second or first, and they seldom reach the posted speed limit, even on flat ground. Also like horses, VW vans are unpredictable. They need constant attention and can sense your feelings. You can't let them know you're afraid. In spite of all this, there's a reason VW vans are so popular. Their imperfections and unpredictability allow travel on a more human level. Cars now are hermetically sealed from the outside world and are driven in complete detachment. Vans put us back in the story.

SANTA BARBARA

Our trip began with coffee in Santa Barbara only a few miles from where we live. Santa Barbara makes me feel poor. And fat. It's an abusive relationship. Because it's so close I often go to one of its cafés to write. And whether it's 10 a.m. or 2 p.m., I know the place will be crowded with beautiful men and women in yoga pants. I'm always suspicious because they're never sweating. In fact, I've come to believe people in Santa Barbara do not sweat. All the sweaty people are herded and shipped to my town. (I also assume that if Santa Barbarans ever do sweat, it smells like seawater spritz and lavender.) Native Santa Barbarans are like wood elves. They have magical powers to stay beautiful for an unnaturally long time. If you see one, you should try to capture him or her.

Despite my feelings, I'm inspired every time I go there. Every block transports me to another time and place where no one works and friends enjoy long conversations over cappuccinos and farm-to-table salads. The buildings have an old-world charm with clay-tile roofs and white stucco walls. Everything is inspirational: the streets, the buildings, the art, the Mexican food. I eat like locals but the food has a different effect on my body.

Santa Barbara is like the girl in high school who is destined to be a movie star. I'm like a kid who'd had classes with her since grade school. She'd always say hello, but when I finally worked up the nerve to talk to her, she called me by the wrong name. I know I'm in an abusive relationship with Santa Barbara, but still I come back. Sometimes I can't even say why. I think it's for the guacamole.

CENTRAL CALIFORNIA WINE COUNTRY

Over a low ridge of coastal mountains to the north of Santa Barbara is a vineyard where my wife and I once rented a home for a weekend. I'm not a big wine drinker and don't know a lot about the various wines, but I've developed a simple system for grading them. As varieties are poured and wine tasters make notes regarding subtle differences and what meals each variety of wine should be paired with, I draw happy faces. The scale goes from one to four, with four happy faces being the top of my scale because to reach five it would have to be beer.

My first wine-country experience was on our honeymoon. We explored country roads near Paso Robles that led to tasting rooms where they never filled the glass enough. I was told you needed only a swig to properly assess the taste, but it was hard to get the honeymoon vibes I was looking for with only a swig.

Everywhere were scenes of flowing red wines and flowers and artisan cheese. It was late spring and mustard grasses blanketed hills, surrounding pockets of oaks with skirts of deep yellow. I learned quickly there was a language of wine. You were supposed to say things such as, "I enjoy the suppleness and fruit-forward flavors of plums and blackberries with occasional hints of mint and cocoa." You were not to say things such as, "Dude, this tastes way better than Bud Light."

We now visit central California wine country often, and this trip connected dots between favorite vineyards from south to north before ending in Big Sur. We began in Los Olivos with our favorite tasting room, Carhartt Vineyard. They call it "the World's Smallest Tasting Room." The intimate patio felt like a friend's backyard. Music floated under wisps of trees growing along the perimeter of the wooden deck. My wife did a flight tasting, a sample of several current offerings poured in order from lighter to richer wines. I had a tall glass of the pourer's favorite red and skipped the flight and the awkward moment where I had to pretend I could taste the difference between them. The wine was called Foreplay, which got four happy faces on name alone. I appreciated the honesty.

My wife and I sat in handcrafted furniture made from warm woods repurposed from old wine barrels. Sometimes we talked about wines, but mostly we talked about life. Summer plans and Christmas lists. Goals and dreams. Kids. The best conversations are paired with slowly poured wine.

After the tasting we drove deeper into the winding, hilly roads of wine country. The light diffused in misty plumes along hilltops and lay heavy in the valleys. The air felt like song. Silence of crisp winds gave way to roosters and birds, the industrious buzzing of bees, and the low-geared humming of tractors on neighboring fields. The earth was patterned. As the day grew, tension of heat was tempered by cooling Pacific winds directed through west-facing valleys. The hills lay low, rolled smooth in short spring grasses and dotted with oaks. The view is a Tuscan sky in California light.

CAMBRIA

The coastal village of Cambria unfolded along a creek between pine-covered knolls. Sidewalks were lined with galleries and cafés and a family market with fresh fruit and vegetables so abundant they spilled from wooden crates. The only change in the ten years since our last visit was the change in us. There was no honeymoon rush. We knew each other's skin and were interested in the deeper beauty discovered in lingering walks along the shore. In youth everything is fast. In maturity time is measured by outgoing tides and the gradual collecting of gifts from the sea.

The day pulled us along with reluctance. A sunrise stroll along Moonstone Beach merged into coffee at the Cambria Coffee Roasting Company that merged into a shoreline picnic of wine and cheese and locally picked fruit. We napped in the van, on a bluff above the ocean with sounds of seabirds and the constant percussion of rolling waves. With the next low tide, we walked again along the shore and looked for sea glass. There was no hurry. The best gifts are always waiting.

BIG SUR

The southern end of Big Sur lumbers from the ocean. It's a land of wild grasses flowing in bays of rolling hills between mountain and sea. In soft Pacific winds grasses fold and ripple like ocean waves. Evidence of a harsher wind is in the trees. Forests of Monterey pines appear hunched with backs turned to the ocean as if bracing for a storm. I could imagine winter squalls, gray and angry, finding landfall, but on that day the views were as agreeable as any. I half expected a hobbit to appear, whistling between puffs on his pipe. Instead, we found a sea-lion rookery and watched mothers teach their young to swim. Beyond the grasses and hills, the mountains rose dangerously, but along the shore the land was humble and quiet.

That all changed past Ragged Point to the north. Along the Big Sur section of Highway 1, mountains and ocean became curves of tangled land and water. Waves pulsed rhythmically, carving at the stone. The view is of two opposites, each magnificent in its own right, but together something utterly amazing. Fresh water falls from forested cliffs directly to the sand, where rocks rise from the sea with stripes of barnacles at the high-tide mark. In its clashing are formed arches and sea stacks and a diversity of life not found anywhere else. The beauty comes in the opposites.

When I first met my wife I tried to win her affection in the same way I won that of friends and admirers—through bold acts of masculinity and a well-edited version of myself. I took her to the nicest restaurants I could afford. I introduced her to influential friends. I told her about my grand plans and assured her of my future success. She wasn't impressed. She loved the little things, the details, such as the thoughtfulness of opening a door or simply holding hands. A woman's heart is not won by strength or masked truth. It's won by poetry. A handful of wildflowers and a bottle of her favorite wine, even if you prefer beer. If you want to truly be a man, study the heart of a woman. It is the landscape we were made to travel.

We parked the van and turned back the covers on our camping bed. Love improves with age, as does love making. It comes from the slow discovery of one's spouse and from being slowly discovered. It would have been a shame to waste the van experience on youthful lust, when I didn't know anything at all about love.

An anniversary is the annual celebration of a daily heroic choice. The choice to prize one's spouse above work or kids or stray lust or friends or hobbies or busyness or our differences. After ten years I've found the battles to elevate my wife above other pursuits in life to be consistently hard. I've also found the rewards to be dramatically improved. In the tangled curves of Big Sur, under silvery shadows of Monterey pines, a beauty is created in the back of a VW van. It is worthy of the wait. An enduring love, able to guide us through turbulent days to the end of this life.

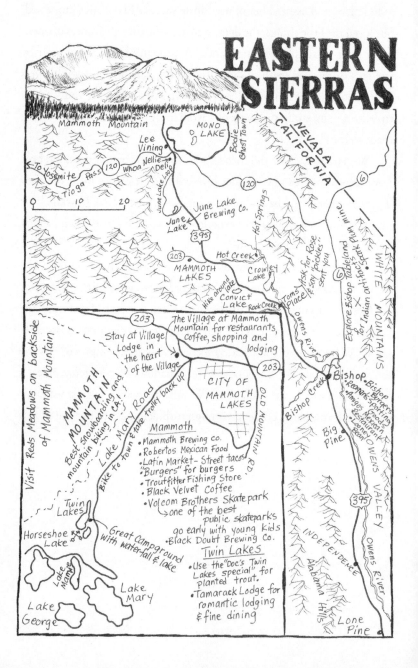

16

Between the Deep Breaths

Eastern Sierras, California

The boys dashed through the front door, and Logan struggled to stand. His tail thumped slowly. It once beat like a metronome; now it labored to move. His hips quivered as he shifted weight to his back paws. The boys gave him a quick pat on the head and ran to their room to play. Logan ambled after them, slipping occasionally under the strain of walking. Upon reaching their room, he nuzzled their necks and licked their faces and returned to the hall where he could keep watch over the boys and the rest of the house.

Since their birth, Logan has always been the first to welcome our boys home. He sniffed newborn hair and retrieved baby toys and rolled over gently when they crawled toward him. I trained him to keep his eyes on me, to wait for my instruction. So when babies climbed his back and tugged his ears, he looked at me as if asking what came next. I told him it was okay, so he let them tug.

Years were marked by his nose's appearance in photos of kids blowing out candles. He was a horse when they played cowboys, and he wore a football helmet when they needed an extra player for the big game. He was a faithful companion. I had no idea how to tell my boys that Logan would have to be put down. That the cancer had grown too strong. That he wouldn't be around for our summer camping trip.

We pulled the boys out of school early to say good-bye. They tried to speak between the deep breaths. Between the clogged air and tears. "Why, Daddy? Why does Logan have to die?"

✕

Wildflowers faded into warm winds of summer and with the last bell of the school year, kids burst from campus with the urgency of a prisoner escape. We prepared for the camping trip to Twin Lakes, near Mammoth, California. In the space where Logan once slept, we packed fishing poles and skateboards. Sadness lingered. I hoped this would be a trip of healing. I hoped forests and rivers and waterfalls would act as sutures.

Loss is not easily mended. We are told to bury our losses, to move on, to fill the hole where a tree has been felled from our life. I wanted to plant a new tree in the space of the loss, but a new tree won't grow until the stump and deep roots of the felled one return to earth. In time, the old tree becomes nourishment for the new.

While we drove to Twin Lakes, the boys asked if we could get a puppy. Could we get him on the trip or when we got home?

"Why, Daddy? Why can't we just go get another dog?"

My heart ached. I could hear the pain in their questions, and they wanted the pain to go away. I wanted that for them too. I wanted to believe a quick trip to the animal rescue or a breeder would make the pain go away.

"I promise, boys, that someday we will, but not right now."

The eastern flank of the Sierra Nevada mountains rises like a gray castle wall. Monoliths stand in defense against vehicles and ambition, and the interior wilderness remains navigable only by trail. The wilderness is filled with an immense glory—alpine lakes and dense forests, remote watersheds and glaciers sitting in the shade of granite mountaintops. There is great reward for anyone willing to enter the glory that few of us penetrate.

Twin Lakes sits at the base of Mammoth Mountain. It is the first of a string of lakes ascending into high elevations of the Sierras. It's shaped like a long, skinny balloon pinched in two places where water flows under small, picturesque bridges. Before reaching the campground, we enjoyed the view of lakes and bridges and the 250-foot Twin Falls cascading from Lake Mamie. Beyond the lodgepole pine and shorelines and waterfalls is a wall of interconnected granite peaks and spires and domes still outlined with snow in early summer.

On the water, men and boys fished in aged aluminum boats numbered along their bows and slick with algae below waterlines. We entered the campground past the first lake, past the warm woods and white linen tablecloths of Tamarack Lodge, and past the general store. We settled into our campsite and went fishing.

I rigged my boys' spinning rods with an adjust-a-bubble float strung between two swivels to keep it from slipping and a Doc Twin Lakes Special streamer purchased at the general store. We anchored near the base of the waterfall and cast into deep waters. Almost immediately, one son's rod doubled over. He panicked with the first jerks, then settled into the careful give and take of reeling in a fish. In a couple of hours, our stringer was full of pan-sized trout to cook over a campfire for dinner.

As we approached the camp, the shore near our campsite erupted with shouts and banging of pots and pans. "Bear! Bear! Bear!"

We saw it racing toward us along the shoreline. The bear was less than twenty feet away, and the only thing between me and the bear was my son. I gripped a canoe paddle with one hand, reached for my knife with the other, and watched as the bear approached at full speed. Its black fur waved front to back, shoulder muscles shuddering with every pounce forward. On all fours it stood as tall as my son, and we could hear grunting and wheezing with its heavy stride.

Above the sounds of the bear's running and the clatter made by other campers, another noise arose. It was the sound of a barking dog. Or better put, it was the sound of yapping. The bear passed us in full panic followed by a poodle yapping at its heels. When our hearts settled we laughed at the sight and reminded each other of the time Logan barked at a bear. The memory moved our hearts to sadness.

We gathered in the living room to tell the boys about Logan. From his favorite spot between us, Logan raised his head when anyone said his name. And when we cried, he tried to raise his body. When his hind legs failed, he placed his front paw on whomever sat nearest. He looked sad. It was the look he gave from the window as he watched us load suitcases into the car.

The boys tried to say good-bye, but had no experience. They looked to me for help, with hearts crushed by feelings they didn't understand, and I knew someday they would understand. They would know a harder world, and even then it would never be easier. I didn't know how to help.

"It's time."

I moved toward Logan, and my boys threw their trembling bodies over him in an effort to protect him. I tried to explain that it wasn't fair for him to remain in pain any longer.

"We'll take care of him, Daddy. Don't take him away."

There are no books or blogs or blueprints to prepare a father's heart for breaking the hearts of his children. I thought about putting this off until the following day or the day after that. Then I pulled the boys gently away and placed them in their mother's lap. I bent low to scoop Logan from the floor, and he grunted in pain. I held his limp body close and he looked at me and his eyes were brown and deep with love. He licked my neck, and I carried him to the side van door. I could hear the boys crying, and I saw his ears perk toward the cries as I laid him in the bed I had made with his favorite blanket.

In the stale light of the veterinary operating room I could see every imperfection of Logan's age. The gray hairs on furrow and brow. The scars from tumors removed. I watched the vet find a vein, and I held Logan's paw and caressed his head as he winced from the pain of the needle. I told him everything would be okay as the vet pushed in the cold medicine. Logan trusted me as he always did. The doctor left us alone.

"Remember how much you loved the water? I would get so mad at you when you would jump into the river at the spot where I was trying to fish. But you knew I wasn't really mad."

I put my forehead against his so my eyes would be the last thing he saw on this earth. His breath was warm and slow. I tried to be as strong for him as he had been for me when my wife and I lost our first pregnancy. And when I lost my best friend. He gave me his paw, and I held it and I rubbed in the place he liked behind his ears. I told him how much the boys and his mom would miss him. I told him how much I loved him.

He kept his eyes on me, and at first they looked confused and then they looked like love. He tried to keep them open. He tried to keep his eyes on me as if asking what came next. I told him it was okay. He closed his eyes, and his warm breath went cold.

I held his paw and limp body and all the warmth that was left. I wanted his eyes to open, for him to nuzzle my neck or to get the ball. Shards of a broken heart pushed through my body, and the pain was beyond bearing. Tears fell, heavy with memory. I kept my eyes on him, asking what was next. I removed his collar and scratched behind his ears and walked out over linoleum tiles swabbed clean with my tears.

I went home to a family that needed me to be a father.

While our boys were young, my wife did most of the parenting, and I did most of the playing. This was the first moment where I had to step up. There were real questions about pain and evil and a fallen world. The answers had consequence. I explained what I could and there was much I could not.

"I'm sorry, boys. I don't have an answer."

But in the woods that summer with the bear and the poodle, I had something greater. Confidence. When life fills with turmoil and change, it's good to return to something that doesn't change. The mountains will always be there. So will the waterfall and the lake and the deep hole where we caught fish last year and the year before that. There is a safety in big things. Throughout life we could always return to this lake in the Eastern Sierras and cast our hurts in the deep waters where a tug on the line would restitch our hearts and the pain would be a reminder that we once loved.

I got a lot of advice about what to do after Logan died. I was told this was a great opportunity to explain the apologetics of how sin entered the world. That sin is the reason we experience pain and suffering and how it's not really God's fault, because of sin. Others told me to get a puppy.

Fathering comes somewhere between the deep breaths and the blank page where there is no script. What my boys needed to know was the truth—that I hurt along with them. They needed to know a father's heart is a broken one, that it's been mended stronger, and as a result has strength to carry any of the pain they cannot. It's only through loss that we can know about healing.

While pain has no subtlety, joy delights in surprise. It snuck up on us in the form of fish. The more we caught, the less we thought about anything else. In the shadow of healing mountains, we giggled and splashed each other with water. The boys asked less about getting a puppy and talked more about what they loved in Logan. I don't know how to describe heaven, but I imagine there will be a lake and a waterfall and a deep hole full of trout. And when we come ashore, we'll be greeted with the cold nose and warm tongue of a golden retriever. His tail will thump against soft earth, and when we bend low his body will curl and circle our legs, and he'll nuzzle into our necks, making sure we are safe. Then he will show us the way home.

THEODORE ROOSEVELT
NATIONAL PARK

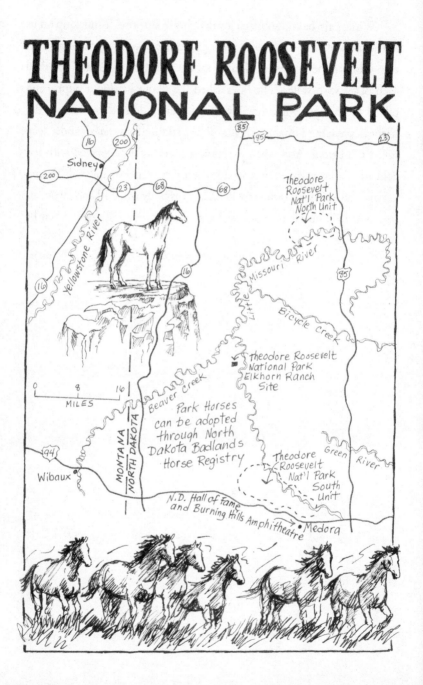

Sidney

Yellowstone River

Theodore Roosevelt Nat'l Park North Unit

Missouri River

Little Missouri River

Bicycle Creek

Theodore Roosevelt National Park Elkhorn Ranch Site

Beaver Creek

Park Horses can be adopted through North Dakota Badlands Horse Registry

Green River

Theodore Roosevelt Nat'l Park South Unit

MONTANA
NORTH DAKOTA

0   8   16
MILES

Wibaux

N.D. Hall of Fame and Burning Hills Amphitheatre

Medora

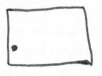

17

Lord of the Badlands

Theodore Roosevelt National Park, North Dakota

I first saw him silhouetted on a bluff above the Little Missouri River. From that height he could survey great distances. Even standing, he appeared to be in motion. His mane blew like a weathervane in shifting winds, his legs authoritative and ready, defined for speed. Atop his sturdy, stiffened neck sat a large head outlined by jowls cut in a half arc and muzzle protruding into the wind.

With the exception of a white stripe on his nose, his face and body were colored in deep chestnut. He is called feral. A wild horse. But he doesn't appear wild or uncontrolled as do most animals. He's dignified and graceful. Powerful as the plains. He's a mythic creature of the North Dakota Badlands. I snuck around the bluff to take a closer look, and he was gone, disappeared into the twilight.

We were told it would be a stroke of good fortune to spot a wild horse. They are described in terms of ghosts. They appear for a moment to graze or look upon the landscape and then vanish before you can reach for a camera to prove you saw one. On a back road of Theodore Roosevelt

National Park, deep into the Badlands, we came across a band of feral horses. They knew we were coming long before we arrived. Their heads cocked slightly, ears perked. They were giving us a gift, a moment with an enduring legend of the North American continent. The hairs on our necks tingled. We felt gospel in the air.

I'd always wanted to travel to North and South Dakota. Primarily because in my mind they are still the Dakota Territories, and a territory represents freedom from a boxed-in world. I spent a lot of time daydreaming about what it would be like when we got to the Badlands. Massive plains. Seas of switchgrass bent in a steady breeze. I'd imagined standing in the loneliness of tall-grass prairies, comforted by subtle sounds of creation and warm scent of earth. I'd imagined my VW van as part of a great wagon train, moving my family across an unsettled West, seeking homestead in lands with smells of undiscovered forests. I'd even imagined my van as a galloping horse (this part takes a lot of imagination) at unrestrained speeds with nothing but hurricane sounds of hooves kicking up scents of prairie sage and a fine plume of dust. I'd imagined we might be visited by Indians.

Visiting a territory is a massively more exciting adventure than visiting a state. To get my kids excited about the trip, I broke out a map and started selling them on the geographic features of the distant country.

"Look how far it is from home." And "We'll be like Lewis and Clark on an epic adventure." And "It's one of the least densely populated and most remote areas of the country." And "What do you guys think?"

"Does it have Wi-Fi?"

I realized it would be a very long drive.

The band of wild horses had a dominant male stallion, bigger than the mares. He communicated through snorting and body movements, but we understood him clearly. He let us know how close we could come to the horses in his watch. We got close enough to *feel* his presence. It was more than sights and sounds or any other senses. I'd had a similar feeling standing next to people I admired, knowing I was outclassed. It's the feeling that causes you to stand at attention, almost unwillingly, as if the presence of a better being is drawing out a better version of yourself. This is how I felt near the stallion. He had an air of majesty—lord of the Badlands.

My family and I are tethered. Beholden to work, to electronic devices, to the pressures put on us from others. As the father, I'm to blame because I have set the tone. I tell the kids they can play video games while I'm sneaking in a little extra work. I text at the dinner table. The world of men is created with boxes. We fence in the property. We build a box and put a roof on it and subdivide the outer box with smaller and smaller interior boxes until eventually our life is defined by what's stored in the closet. When we spend too much time in our boxes, we become controlled by the things we've created. The only way I know to break free is to seek the expansive, the untamed.

As the name suggests, the Badlands are untamable. They are a grand network of fissures in the earth. It's a broken land, but beauty is most often found in broken places. Grasses give way to fragmented forms of sandstone, erratically carved over an age by the Little Missouri River. The land falls away, disappearing into mystery. All approaches into the eroded landscape follow a route through downward-terraced sediment. Water has carved the land into intricate columns and buttes and rock faces that, in the spell of moonlight, look like ruins of ancient cities. It's a place to be lost.

Surrounding the Badlands are the great northern plains. For as long as there have been people on this continent, the plains have provided for them. In exchange for its abundance, it has endured exploitation. From the near-extermination of free-range bison and the government's break-ing of treaties with Native Americans, to the constant pressure of frack-ing for oil, the land is like Shel Silverstein's *The Giving Tree* and is suffering a similar fate. We have taken the wild game. Taken the territory. Taken its oil. We are defined by what we consume. I wish I had some-thing to offer in return. Passing through the plains I try to think of a worthy offering, but land beats me to it. It offers our family peace, a time to be together without distraction.

My kids feel it too, though it comes through strict restrictions on the use of mobile devices. Like any addiction, its breaking is severe. But wide-open land breaks the spell. What before seemed boring now becomes an adventure. Their imaginations go wild with Indians and bison and wild horses. They ask bigger questions. Then they're quiet, sitting for miles in sacred silence. No devices. No empty words.

As we look out windows in any direction, the earth moves like water. We are near the middle of the North American continent, and I can feel it. It's the gravity of our land's generosity pulled to the center. This gener-osity is as wide as the plains and is given as a gift. Again I wish I had something to offer in return; I want to be defined by what I give. But we can be defined by what we give only if we are free from what we consume. I mostly take.

The wild horses perform as they were created to. They run for pleasure, to feel wind through their manes and to smell earth passing underfoot. They cover great distances and on any day might be found miles from where they were seen a day before. Their power is found in their freedom. All created beings are under the authority of what they fear. Wild horses are not controlled by it. They are not fearful of money or what a family member or friend might say about them. There is nothing in their domain they fear, except maybe us. They can sense we were created with a higher purpose.

The national park was named for Theodore Roosevelt, who came to hunt the Dakota Territory in his pursuit of becoming a man. He purchased property and entrenched himself in the western life of hunting and ranching. The ruggedness and barren beauty of the Badlands convinced him that the area, and lands similar, needed protection from a developing country with commercial priorities. His formative experiences in the Badlands greatly influenced his conservation policies. The land and the animals in it made him better. They made and continue to make the country better. If we let it, they will make us better too.

As stunning as the landscape is, it's the image of wild horses that completes it. The stallion is resting. His body is a form of pleasing right angles. While his nose is pointed toward earth his eyes are fixed constantly on the horizon. He reads the land. When he looks my direction, I feel he is reading me as well. My soul is stirred. I want to live in the same freedom and have the same power define me.

Seeing the wild horses created a before and an after in my life. They unlocked change within me. They are a haunting image to call upon when I lose sight of freedom.

I think often of the northern plains, filled only with good earth and sky and distant wind. I think about the prairie winds parting manes of wild horses and the stallion in the switchgrass reading me with his soul-eyes. I'm not sure I'll ever see any of it again. I read about a constant pressure to take more from the land. About drilling and pipelines to fuel our nation's consumption. Then I realize what I can give back. My gift would be to live in the freedom offered. To consume less. To take less. To participate in the restoration of damaged lands and to live responsibly within them. I've been told that heaven is a reflection of a perfectly restored earth. I imagine there we will ride wild horses.

Zen and the Art of Vanagon Maintenance, Part I

Mariposa, California

Every year we camp in Yosemite National Park with our closest friends, and though it's mostly noncompetitive camping, I've grown competitive about it. My natural instincts lie less toward wilderness survival and more toward making hand crafts that involve pinecones. But with each trip I have worked harder at trying to impress with new camping skills.

On our family's last trip, I got the attention of Greg and the other guys in our group. "Hey guys, watch me make kindling with my new axe!" I'm making progress, but I'm still not there.

Brady unloads his already perfectly cut kindling, and Scott whips out an axe he most likely fashioned himself from raw materials passed down from ancestral New Hampshire forests. Meanwhile, Dave heads toward the camper, where I'm pretty sure he stashes a chain saw. I look sadly at my new axe. I think it was made in China. Or Brooklyn.

But this year is different. I have a 4WD VW Westfalia camper van and will be rolling into Yosemite in serious retro-cool camping style. In previous years I stumbled awkwardly into camp with my wife and kids in an eighties-era motor home (a.k.a. The Death Star) and later on in our trusty hand-me-down Suburban, complete with gear obtained at outdoor superstores such as Target and Walmart. But this year we made a late start from home so we could maximize the grandness of our arrival at the campground. I'd been daydreaming about the guys standing around my new van toasting with longneck beers when my wife startled me from my van-zen with a question.

"Is the red light supposed to be blinking?"

"Oh yeah, that's totally normal."

I have no idea what the red light is for. My instinct tells me a blinking red light is probably a bad thing. That doesn't keep me from also trying to convince myself it's normal.

We've been driving for an hour and a half, but since we're in a VW van, we've traveled only forty miles and are on a section of Interstate 5 known as The Grade. It's a steep, hot climb, and the shoulder of the road is littered with overheated vehicles. When I purchased this van, the size of the windshield was one of the zen elements used to sell an otherwise bad idea. Now, with the windshield filled with a four-lane vertical wall, the zen is slipping through the never-quite-sealed cracks in the windows.

The blinking of the red light began slowly, like a casual wink. I imagined the blinks as a secret van language code.

Hey dude, you should at some point check out the engine. Whenever you want, man. It's all good.

But then the blinking became steady and added a loud buzz that cut rudely through the Bob Marley CD I was playing. Next to the red blinking light was the heat gauge. It was pegged on high.

Just kidding about that, bro. You need to pull over now. You're totally screwed.

My wife wanted to know how bad it was. I told her it was no big deal. It's an old engine and just needed to cool down. I said it calmly because at that point she still believed I knew more about the van engine than she did. We were still within the two-hundred-mile towing range of our AAA membership. A sensible decision would have been to get towed home, throw our stuff in the Suburban, and continue with the trip. But I knew The Grade well and we were near the top. So instead of pulling over, I made the nonsensible decision to continue the trip in the van. Proving that I am, after all, a man.

After cresting the grade I put the transmission in neutral and coasted the next twenty miles. The temperature gauge went to low and all systems were go.

"See, honey, everything is fine."

And for a while everything was fine.

We approached the bridge in Kingsburg overlooking a stretch of the Kings River, and I knew we'd gone two hundred miles because I have a map marked with all the places we can go and still get towed home. It had been several hours since the engine overheated, and I'd been lulled back into my van-zen groove. Then at 201 miles I saw it.

The red light was blinking. I didn't look at it, hoping it would go away. My wife finally noticed the warning light outside Fresno. I told her it'd been going on for a while, but the temperature was fine, and we'd just keep an eye on the gauge. The kids were asleep and we shouldn't wake them. Plus, I had rerouted the trip; instead of going over the high passes of Highway 41, we'd go the long way around on Highway 140 and follow the river into The Park.

"As long as we take it easy, it won't be a problem. All we had to do last time was wait for the engine to cool down. How much worse could it get?"

On the first foothill my wife saw smoke from the engine. The red light screamed at me, my wife wanted answers, and my kids asked if the van was on fire. As I pulled off the road the rear of the van was engulfed in smoke. Fluid came from everywhere. Oil and coolant and water and who knows what else were leaking out. I was 80 percent certain there would be an explosion, so we hid behind tree trunks. There was no explosion, which was a disappointment for everyone.

With camping gear strapped to every possible location, the van looked like a pack animal. The engine's in the rear of the van, and gaining access required unloading bikes and coolers and chairs. I half expected a kitchen sink. With our stuff strewn along the side of the highway, we looked more like flea-market vendors than hipster campers. I looked at the engine. It's a mystery of metal and hoses. My older son inspected the engine with me.

"What's wrong with it, Daddy?"

I had no idea what to tell him. I have memories of breaking down with my dad and his fixing whatever was wrong and getting his family safely back on the road. I know lots of men like this, and they all seem greater than me. In these moments I wish I could be *that* guy. The hero of the story. The guy who can fix an engine on the side of a road.

"I don't know what to do, Son. Let's say a quick prayer and call for help."

The tow truck arrived. The driver was my age, and though we were similar in size, his build was defined by mountains and hard labor. His hat had a sharp crease in the bill with an Above All Towing logo embroidered on the front. We shook hands. His grip was firm, but there was gentleness in his eyes and voice.

"How can I help you folks?"

I explained the situation as best I could, and after inspecting the engine he gave his assessment. "You have a busted hose connector."

I quickly chimed in, "Yep, that's what I was thinking."

He said he could fix it right there. Of course he could. He listed a couple of parts and tools he clearly expected I'd be carrying. I had nothing beyond some crafting supplies designed for working on pinecones. So we loaded the van onto the tow truck.

After the disappointment of not seeing an explosion, my boys were excited to be riding in a tow truck and climbed into the backseat with my wife. I sat up front and tried to make small talk as we drove back to Mariposa.

I asked the driver, "Do you like to fish?"

"Yes sir. I like to go noodling."

"Noodling? What's that?"

"You hunt for giant catfish holes, and instead of using bait, you shove your arm in the hole and wiggle your finger like a worm. When the catfish swallows your arm you yank it out. Or you drown."

"Oh," I said. "I like to fish with tiny flies."

✕

It's early fall. Oaks are shedding in umbers and reds. The Sierra Nevada foothills appear as a rumpled quilt. The town of Mariposa sits quietly in a crevice of these folds. Streets are lined with historic stone and wooden storefronts dating to the town's founding at the peak of California's gold rush. While the van was being repaired, we shopped along boardwalks and sipped coffee on the patio of the Pony Expresso. The tow truck driver recommended the local pizza place. When we shared our story with the manager, she bought our lunch. We were almost saddened to leave when we got the mechanic's call that our van was ready to get back on the road.

Climbing in I was unnerved that twice now the van broke down and I didn't know what to do to fix it. One of my greatest struggles has been my inability to fix anything mechanical. There's a deep-rooted sense in all men that they should be able to fix things. To protect their family. To get out of a jam. Every time I call for help a piece of manhood is carved from my soul, and I begin to believe I'm something less. When I was younger, I suppressed these emotions with rationalizations that, since my dad died before teaching me about cars, I wasn't obligated to learn about them. But now I have kids, and the rationalizations ring hollow as a heart without truth.

Back on the road I was thankful that the van was fixed, our bellies were full, and we were driving into the sunset. We crested the first large hill and my confidence rose. From previous travels I knew there were a couple more hills and then it was downhill to the river followed by a gentle rise into The Park.

"See, honey, everything's going to be fine."

The blinking red light reappeared.

My wife suggested we turn and coast back to Mariposa. No way. This was probably just a malfunction with the light. The van was fine. It was just the devil taunting us with his blinking light.

Going up the next grade things got worse. The light didn't stop blinking, and now it was joined by sounds of clanking metal. The sun had set. It was dark. I continued on. We were on a steep mountain incline, and even the kids wondered if we should turn around. Nope. Then came the buzzing. We had almost reached the top of a long grade. Then came the smoke. There was one last plea for me to turn around.

"No! We're at the top of the hill. We can coast all the way into The Park."

Everybody went silent. As we crested the hill, the engine seized. Everything was dark. Everything except the blinking light.

Had we turned around we could have coasted all the way to Mariposa. We could have left the van at the repair shop and returned to the coffee shop or the pizza place or a hotel. Instead, the van descended into a deep, dark hole. With it I descended into every shallowly buried doubt about my masculinity and myself. Every twist in the dark came as a dagger to my heart.

We coasted for a ways into the flat and pulled off the highway, rolling to a stop in a protected cove of canyon wall. I tried one last time to start the engine, and it gave a whimper and a thud. The blinking light was gone.

My older son was first to break the silence. "This is the darkest night of my life."

He wanted to know if I knew how to fix it. I really wished at that moment I could tell him what tool to hand me and we could fix the van together and heal this masculine wound I carry. But I could no more fix the engine than my son could understand my need to fix it.

"We'll be okay," I told him.

"How do you know?"

We said a quick prayer, and I reached for the phone and called for help. A tow truck was dispatched.

Minutes later a car traveling the opposite direction stopped on the far side of the highway. I crossed over and they offered to call a tow truck when they got to the next town. I told them a tow truck was on the way.

"Wow, that's a miracle!"

I asked why.

"There's never cell reception in this canyon."

I looked at my phone, and sure enough it didn't have reception.

"Well, God bless you guys." They drove off.

When their taillights disappeared in the curve of the canyon, I was surrounded by the quiet of mountains. Just beyond I could hear for the first time the gentle swirl of the Merced River, the same river that helped carve the granite of Yosemite Valley where our friends were sleeping that night. I knew with a call in the morning they would pick us up and make space for my family in tents and vans and welcome us with clanking of longneck beers. Looking to the stars and beyond, I felt the deep peace of night descend on me. I returned to where my boys were sleeping in the van, nestled safely in the canyon's embrace.

Soon lights flashed in the canyon, and I saw an Above All tow truck headed our way. I was reassured. There is something Above All. And He can be trusted. And maybe my sons saw something at work today more important than me fixing an engine.

I met the tow truck driver at the rear of the van, and he pointed to the river gurgling in the dark.

"Did you catch any fish with your tiny flies?"

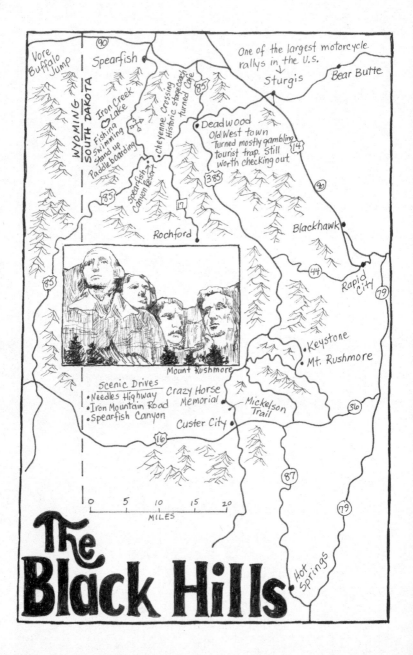

Vore Buffalo Jump

Wyoming / South Dakota

90

Spearfish

Iron Creek Lake
Fishing
Swimming
Stand up
Paddleboarding

Spearfish Canyon Resort

85

Cheyenne Crossing
Historic Stagecoach Turned Cafe

85

One of the largest motorcycle rallys in the U.S.
→ Sturgis

Bear Butte

Deadwood
Old West town
Turned mostly gambling tourist trap. Still worth checking out.

14

385

90

17

Rochford

Blackhawk

44

85

Rapid City

79

Mount Rushmore

Keystone
Mt. Rushmore

Scenic Drives
• Needles Highway
• Iron Mountain Road
• Spearfish Canyon

Crazy Horse Memorial

Mickelson Trail

36

Custer City

16

87

0 5 10 15 20
MILES

79

Hot Springs

The Black Hills

19

Passing into Legend

The Black Hills, South Dakota

first heard about the Black Hills from my grandfather. Once he broke free from the bonds of Depression-era poverty, he began to explore the world. With my grandma, he traveled every continent, with the exception of Antarctica, and every corner of our country. I picked up Grandpa's wanderlust and have taken every opportunity to travel throughout our country and abroad, though my heart is in the West. He and I spent a lot of time discussing the various places we'd both traveled, and those places we still wanted to explore. Our discussions about different places and destinations gave me a chance to slip in areas of life where I needed advice or encouragement. Most of the time, Grandpa just seemed to know what I needed to hear.

We'd be in a coffee shop, talking. "Why don't you get a scone with that?"

"I can't, Grandpa. I'm on a diet."

"Why are you on a diet?"

To emphasize the point I grabbed my belly, generously, with both hands. As a way to either mock or mirror me, Grandpa grabbed his belly, also with both hands, and shook it vigorously. He had a few more lattes and pecan pies in his.

"This isn't fat," he said. "This is an accomplishment." He paused for a second, figuring out how to best emphasize the point. Then he continued, "A man's gotta build a shed to cover his tools."

Between our travels together and separately we'd covered a good deal of the American West. I asked him about his "must see" places. The Black Hills and Mount Rushmore were on his list and, in particular, the Crazy Horse Memorial. I asked why, having always assumed it was nothing more than a gimmicky tourist area—one of those places you've seen pictures of and once you saw it in person wished you had stuck to the pictures. Like Niagara Falls or Rock City.

"I can't explain why," he said. "You just need to see it."

The Black Hills rise from tall-grass prairies that range from Oklahoma to central Canada. This expanse of grasslands forms the Great Plains. In the middle of these plains, the Black Hills seem out of place. You can circle them and barely change in elevation, yet to drive through them requires traversing mountains higher than any east of the Rocky Mountains. The granite core rises above 7,200 feet and is shaped like a bull's-eye, with concentric rings of pine and spruce descending to the plains.

Traveling from mountains of the West, I am surprised by the Black Hills. From a distance they appear as a dark mist, vision-like. These lands have long been considered sacred. People of the Sioux nation— descendants of those who lived near the Black Hills when the first white settlers arrived—consider them to be the spiritual center of the world. It's where they're meant to pray. The area has been denigrated by human schemes. Reversals of treaties and the scars of quick wealth hang over the hills. Yet the region's spirit endures. Once a place has been marked by God, it becomes eternal.

I entered from the north, through the outlaw-turned-gambling town of Deadwood, from whence we've inherited stories of Wild Bill Hickok and Calamity Jane. The buildings are historic and well preserved, but only a façade. Deadwood is as authentically western as Las Vegas is desert oasis. Past the town, the mountains open up. The highway winds organically, following patterns of rivers and old game trails and has a sense of ease. There are no cliff-climbing grades or brake-burning descents. Just a gracious invitation to be lost in mountains and creeks and thought and wonder.

Crossing other mountains comes with fear and anxiety, wondering if my van will make it or if we have enough food and blankets on hand in case it doesn't. On those crossings my mind is in too many places to be any good. The roads through the Black Hills, in contrast, are perfectly made for my van. I let go of worry and become fully present.

Mountains often are judged by their size. Compared to the Rocky Mountains, or even my own Sierra Nevadas, the Black Hills fall short in this category. They don't have the massive peaks or grand alpine meadows and lakes. In fact, the Black Hills are shrinking with burdens of time. They huddle as an aging man in a blanket keeping his memories warm. The Black Hills don't come with reckless promises and daring feats of youth. These sacred mountains come as wisdom and peace. The thoughtful traveler would be wise to accept both.

$$\times$$

On the southern side of the mountains, I come across the Crazy Horse Memorial. Among the visitors, there is more staring than photo taking. Only the head and general form have been carved out of the massive rock, and it dwarfs the size of the better-known neighbors at Mount Rushmore. Once it is completed, this will be the world's largest sculpture. It's a privately funded project, financed by the donations of visitors and those who want to help call attention to the unfair treatment these tribes have endured at the hands of our government. The indigenous people are still looking for their lands to be returned to them. The face of the monument is noble. Proud. Like the people. I'm moved by the ambition. It's certainly better than a casino.

The scene at Rushmore is a contrast. It's filled with buses and couples in matching jackets. The crowd is quick with photos but slow with curiosity. It's a hive of activity with the most important outcome being one's head inserted into a photo of the monument, as if the person's head also were carved into stone. I wonder how many millions of Americans have a photo in a shoe box showing the time they were photobombed by history.

Washington, Jefferson, Theodore Roosevelt, and Lincoln were chosen as subjects for the memorial because of their unique contributions to the building of our country. Also because the president at the time made the sculptor pick, in addition to Washington, two Republicans and a Democrat. No matter, these men were undoubtedly good men. Maybe even great.

I'm not on a career path that will lead to my head being carved in a mountain. In fact, most of us never will have a monument or statue made for us. We will not be celebrated in poems or movies. My professional achievements will be mostly forgotten upon my death or shortly after. I struggle with the futility of this. I desire to leave a lasting impact on this earth, and I wonder what choices I could have made that might have led to a monument. I wonder what choices are left.

We erect monuments to represent or remind us of ideals of greatness or to honor men and women who have managed to live these ideals. We erect them in steel and stone, bronze and cast iron. But even these won't last forever. At best our monuments will outlast the ideals they represent.

In the shade of our country's forefathers, I'm left to wonder what lasts forever.

I call Grandpa to let him know I'm at Rushmore. He wants to know about the trip and what I'm seeing and learning. I tell him about the monuments and about the roads, and he says he wishes he could be riding his motorcycle through the hills. I lose interest in the stone monuments; I'm talking to the real thing.

A man needs to have carved in the mountains of his heart the great men he will look to when the chips are down. Fathers and grandfathers. Friends and mentors. These men need to be identified and chosen for their character and carved so clearly the character becomes our own. In turn we are chiseled and carved until we resemble the same likeness. This is what lasts forever: character and faith passed from generation to generation until we are restored with our lands. Grandpa is my Crazy Horse. We are the monuments carved upon the hearts of our children.

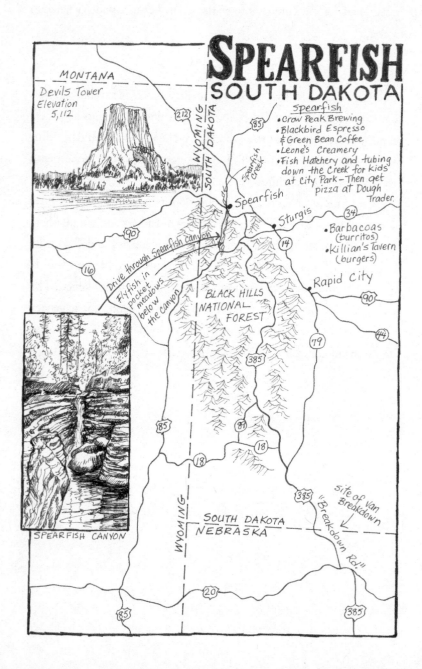

SPEARFISH
SOUTH DAKOTA

MONTANA

Devils Tower
Elevation
5,112

212

WYOMING
SOUTH DAKOTA

85

Spearfish Creek

Spearfish
- Crow Peak Brewing
- Blackbird Espresso & Green Bean Coffee
- Leone's Creamery
- Fish Hatchery and tubing down the creek for kids at City Park - Then get pizza at Dough Trader.

Spearfish

90

Sturgis

34

14

- Barbacoas (burritos)
- Killian's Tavern (burgers)

Rapid City

90

16

Drive through Spearfish canyon
Flyfish in pocket meadows below the canyon

BLACK HILLS NATIONAL FOREST

79

44

385

85

87

18

SPEARFISH CANYON

18

385

WYOMING

SOUTH DAKOTA
NEBRASKA

Site of van Breakdown

"Breakdown Rd!"

20

85

385

20

Zen and the Art of Vanagon Maintenance, Part II

Spearfish Canyon, South Dakota

The red light was flashing and the oil alarm was buzzing and the kids were listening and I was trying to keep it together. I'm not sure where we were—somewhere in South Dakota maybe. Or it could've been Nebraska. There weren't many signs. Or cars.

"Daddy, where are we?"

"I'm not sure."

"Are you going to fix the van?"

I went through motions of fixing the van, mostly for theater so the kids wouldn't lose complete confidence in me. For miles a mutiny had been brewing in the backseat. If I lost it now the inmates would take over. The engine was in the rear of the van, under the storage area, and everybody knew the routine. It's a bucket-brigade process of removing camping gear and sleeping bags to make it possible to get at the engine compartment. I looked at a jumble of metal and wires, not with hopes of identifying the problem but hoping I could be left alone while I fought inner demons assaulting my soul. I just wanted a moment of quiet.

"What's that, Daddy?"

I was like a possum, hoping if I stood still he might go away.

"Daddy, what is it?"

"It's the engine."

My younger son pointed to something more specific.

"What's that, Daddy?"

"That, Son, is the alternator."

I had no idea what it was, or even where he was pointing. I wasn't paying much attention.

"What's that?"

"The starter."

"What's that?"

"A pipe?"

"What's that?"

"The alternator."

"You already said that."

I hate this game.

My older son didn't bother with questions. He walked off to practice his pitching by throwing stones at a rotting fence post. We had pulled off the road near a stagnant pond, and the mosquitoes found blood. My wife stayed busy spraying bug spray and looking for snacks because she knew we'd be here awhile. I hoped my younger son would lose interest, but all he seemed to care about is what some chunk of metal in the engine compartment was for.

"It's a backup alternator."

"Why does the van need a backup?"

"Listen, I'm trying to fix the engine. This is very dangerous. You need to stop asking questions and let me work."

This brought about quiet. I used the time to figure out how to get my family out of yet another van breakdown. The sun was setting and, according to the map, we were about 180 miles from our destination in Spearfish, South Dakota. Since I couldn't fix the engine, the choice was either to tow the van someplace close or tow it someplace far. I decided to have it towed to Spearfish.

"Why is it dangerous?"

I didn't answer. Instead I called a tow truck.

"Why can't you fix it?"

"Go throw rocks with your brother."

The greatest wound a man carries is the shame he bears for the areas where he doesn't see himself as a man. Every man develops this wound. For some it started by dropping a fly ball that allowed the other team to win. For others it's the dropped balls of marriage or kids. For me it's a roadside lie that drills into my soul. It says that not being able to fix an engine is tantamount to incompetency.

My dad could fix anything mechanical. I have great memories of him under the hood of his '57 Chevy truck, arm deep in grease and metal. He had a cigarette that was smoked without hands as if it were another tool. There was grunting and cussing and a cold beer when the engine turned over. This became my vision of a man. He died before I could develop any other. I thought I would somehow learn these things, perhaps as a way to honor his legacy. Alongside the highway, as night approached, I felt I had let us both down.

The shoulder of a highway runs like a heel-drawn line in the dirt. On one side of the line is the man with the courage to repair his brokenness. The man on the other side gets stuck in his shame. All men are on this road trip. There's a beginning and there will be an end, the ending informed by how well we travel. We all get stuck on the shoulder, and sometimes courage is a call for help. There's no shame in rescue. When shame is shared it also is diluted, and a diluted shame has no potency. By repair or rescue, real men get back on the road. A life off the highway is no life at all.

In fading sun a tow truck arrived with a full light display. There was no other traffic on the highway, and I wondered if the flashing lights were necessary. I'm pretty sure the entrance to hell is marked with pulsing red lights and the buzzing of an oil alarm. Lights and sounds of incompetence on earth. The tow-truck driver inspected the engine.

"Are you sure you want a tow? It's just a couple of belts."

My eyes moved from the engine to the horizon to the ground below my feet.

"Yes, I'm sure."

The van was winched onto the truck's bed and the family loaded into the cab. Soon we were driving eighty miles an hour and a thought occurred to me. *This is as fast as the van has ever gone. Maybe we should just take a tow truck across America.*

I could feel the West in the wind. It carried the distance between the man I am and the man I'm still becoming. It bent my heart as it bent the tall grass.

When you grow accustomed to the West, you think of the land as being bordered by mountains. They are the darkened lines that hold the color of emptiness between. But here on the plains, there are no lines. Colors spill off the page, are soaked by sky, and bleed into the sunset. I feel so small, a disappearing dot in a receding landscape. In canyons and mountains you are never fully alone for there is always an echo, a voice returning to you. Voices here on the plains never return. Sound is carried upon august winds, scattered tongues, absorbed by creation. There is no beginning or ending. There is only sky and earth and wind. The empty northern plains feel like infinity.

We traveled forty miles before the driver said anything. "So, you like VW vans?"

$$\times$$

Spearfish lies on the northern slopes of the Black Hills, near the mouth of Spearfish Canyon. Friends of ours moved here recently and talked of how quickly they fell in love with the beauty of these isolated mountains and the friendliness of the people. After a morning tour through a revitalized downtown, it was easy to see the attraction. There's an ease about the community, a comfortableness with itself. I love a town that's not trying to be like some other place. The downtown area was filled with carefully cared for buildings housing locally owned coffee shops and boutiques and purveyors of outdoor recreational equipment. The town was filled with conversation. People asked one another about families and favorite books and escape plans for when the Sturgis Motorcycle Rally would take place.

I had grand plans for our time here but first needed to get the van fixed. My wife and our friend packed a picnic to have lunch between adventures on mountains and lakes and rivers. I ordered lunch at Applebee's. It wasn't far from where a mechanic worked on our van.

"It's just a couple belts," he told me.

"I know. I didn't bring the right tool set."

He looked at me suspiciously and gave me walking directions to several restaurants, of which Applebee's was the best.

I ordered a salad, prompting the waitress to ask where I was from. I guessed her to be the age of my mother. I wanted her name to be Flo, but it wasn't, though I can't remember what it was. Her smile, though, I remember. It was as genuine and great as the plains.

"I'm from California."

"Wow! That's far. What brings you all the way to Spearfish?"

"I heard you had great salads."

"We do! But you should try a steak. They're real good."

"I think I'll just get a salad." I wasn't feeling man enough for steak.

"Oh, no! You can't do that! Honey, you sure you don't want steak?"

We reached a compromise. "I'll have a steak salad."

"They're real good."

The waitress returned often. She asked if I needed more salad dressing or water and where I would be going next. And she wanted to know about my wife and if she liked traveling without a toilet and about the kids and what their ages were and what they liked in school. I liked the companionship, and it felt good to get some things off my chest about the van breaking down.

"Honey, you should always get belts checked before a trip."

I barely had time to pay the bill before the mechanic called to let me know the van was ready. I felt much better after my Applebee's therapy session and struck up a conversation with the repair-shop owner and his wife. They charged about a third of what I expected, fairness I hadn't seen in a while. They're a lovely couple, and we talked about kids and fishing. They suggested a drive through Spearfish Canyon.

Spearfish Creek descends from heights of the Black Hills like a chinook wind. The canyon whispers of a previous age, a sacred time, when people communed with creation. They were drawn to the mountains because language there spoke of a Creator.

No one seemed to speak this language anymore. Motorcycles and buses of tourists sped through the canyon from waterfall to waterfall, with brief stops so people could insert themselves into photos to prove they'd been here. We are not meant to be tourists in this life. We are all travelers, like those before and those after. The proof we've been in a place is the part of us we leave there. We know we've been somewhere special because we are forever different as a result of it.

This land and time are gifts. If we stop long enough, we might hear in the wind the voice of the Creator. We don't have to search for it. It has always been and always will be. We just have to listen long enough to remember the language.

I slipped off the highway to a dirt road along the creek. The creek tumbled recklessly over a small ridge, then gathered for a moment of reverence to reflect the sacred canyon walls. The canyons were layered in limestone and colored in umber and gray with streaks of a red so deep it could be the blood of the mountain. From serpentine canyon walls sprouted ponderosa pines and white spruce, a hue of green to set as a backdrop for the yellows and golds of deciduous aspen. The colors repeated themselves in a rhythmic pattern, from shaded canyon floor to slender strips of blue showing only briefly between thousand-foot walls.

The creek spilled around boulders with swishes and sizzles of current. The pond was lined with grasses and wildflowers, and hiding within these banks I watched ripples of rising trout. The fish in these waters are wild and once were so plentiful they were speared as part of a native diet. The ritual spearing of fish is how the creek and canyon were named. Though no longer plentiful enough to be speared, these wild trout are sought by fishermen from all over the country.

For the better part of a day I had the river and canyon to myself, though I wasn't alone. The voice of the Creator was with me as I cast a line deep below walls of a half-lit canyon. He spoke with assurances that I am more than I think I am. I was assured I'm the hero my boys need. The heroic sacrifice needed is my time, even if it's spent along the shoulder of the highway. I have no pictures of Spearfish Canyon, yet I know I was there. My life is different because of it.

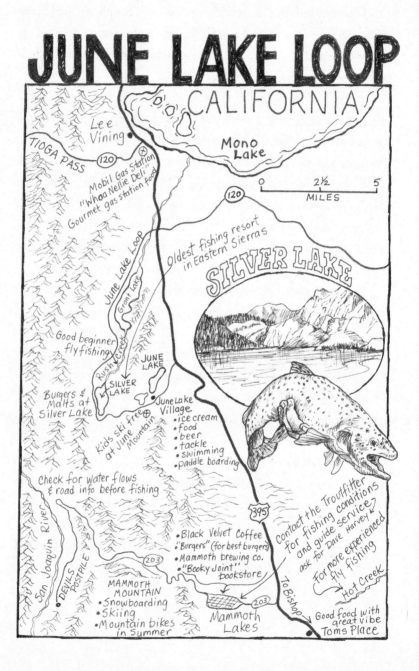

JUNE LAKE LOOP

CALIFORNIA

Lee Vining

Mono Lake

TIOGA PASS

120

Mobil Gas Station
"Whoa Nellie Deli"
Gourmet gas station food

120

0   2½   5
MILES

Oldest fishing resort
in Eastern Sierras

SILVER LAKE

June Lake Loop

Grant Lake

Rush Creek

Good beginner
fly fishing

JUNE LAKE

SILVER LAKE

Burgers &
Malts at
Silver Lake

Kids ski free
at June Mountain

June Lake
Village
• ice cream
• food
• beer
• tackle
• swimming
• paddle boarding

Check for water flows
& road info before fishing

San Joaquin River

DEVILS POSTPILE

203

395

• Black Velvet Coffee
• "Burgers" (for best burgers)
• Mammoth Brewing co.
• "Booky Joint"
   bookstore

Contact the Troutfitter
for fishing conditions
and guide service
ask for Dave Harvey

For more experienced
fly fishing

Hot Creek

MAMMOTH
MOUNTAIN
• Snowboarding
• Skiing
• Mountain bikes
   in Summer

203

Mammoth
Lakes

To Bishop

Good food with
great vibe
Toms Place

Whiskey and Firelight

June Lake Loop, California

June Lake Loop is actually only a half loop. It exits from Highway 395, the main north-south artery along the Eastern Sierras, returning after a fourteen-mile retreat. It's called a scenic loop, but that's a modest designation. Highway 395 is altogether scenic and, in places, astoundingly beautiful. June Lake Loop is like meeting someone you've admired from a distance and finding he or she is even better in person.

It climbs quickly to its namesake, a quaint four-season town known as June Lake. The town is filled with ice-cream shops, fishing stores, and breakfast cafés serving pancakes the size of saucers. Past town is a ski resort and a stretch of road that's often impassible in winter. Mountains close in and the road threads through aspens and lodgepole pines before opening to a high mountain meadow traversed by meandering Rush Creek, which then enters Silver Lake.

Silver Lake lies at the base of all beauty. It's the oldest fishing resort in the Eastern Sierras, with history tasted in every burger and chocolate malt savored after a long day of fishing. From lakeshore, sawtooth peaks soar in every direction, the crevices filled with snow and ribbons of aspen running gold in autumn. Horsetail Falls, fed by alpine lakes and headwaters deep in the Yosemite wilderness, feathers into the valley. Light falls softly, as fresh on skin as a misty waterfall. Water once again focuses at the lake's downstream meadow, turning back into a creek. This is where my friend Chuck and I fished.

We found a promising stretch of water and waded under the canopy of aspens. In the late season water ran thinly, in some places barely topping our boots. Chuck fished a deeper pool fed by water tumbling over boulders and a fallen log. We both knew there'd be a fish there, but though he presented several flies, nothing bit. We tried other sections with similar results until, almost as an afterthought, Chuck cast a line in a six-inch deep riffle at the tail of the pool. The water turned violent, and Chuck's fly rod doubled over on itself.

Though he had fished his whole life, Chuck was new to fly-fishing, and this was the biggest fish he'd hooked on a fly. The shallow riffle became a torrent of activity. The trout turned on itself with tail slapping the surface. Almost instantly water swelled several feet away. The creek looked like war, explosions triggered every few feet. The fish was everywhere at once. It didn't tire.

I encouraged Chuck with some pointers. "Keep the rod tip high. Let it take some line. Lead it toward the bank."

The fish had other ideas. Perhaps his buddy was calling different instructions. "Yank the line. Try to break the knot. Swim around a log a bunch of times."

I didn't have a net on me because earlier experience suggested I didn't need one. You had to catch fish for that. I ran to get the net, splashing and stumbling with all the grace of an elephant on ice. The whole time Chuck fought the trout.

"Keep the line tight," I instructed. "Hold it there. I've got the net."

"Dude, hurry up!"

Chuck is a firefighter, so he's used to running with gear and hoses and is good in emergency situations. I'm a writer and can barely handle an adjective. I grabbed the net, but it was still attached to my gear bag. As I yanked it, gear flew everywhere.

"Are you coming?"

I slipped on a rock. My heart was pounding, not from excitement, but because I'm genuinely out of shape. I made a quick promise to start running again. Or at least to walk briskly to the taco shop.

The fish still hadn't tired. It continued to burst with energy, each time folding Chuck's fly rod in half. I could see it was a wild brown trout by the bright orange spots along its lateral line. It looked to be eighteen inches in length, maybe more, and so thick in the middle I wondered how it fit in the shallow riffle where it was hooked. I got positioned with the net and instructed Chuck to lead the fish toward me. The net didn't seem big enough. I reached for the trout and suddenly the knot attaching the fly to the tippet broke. The rod recoiled and the line whipped back with the sudden release of tension. We stood in the water, stunned, silent as church mice. Chuck broke the silence first.

"Does that count?"

"It does for me."

A great thing about fishing is it justifies consumption of food and beer in amounts disproportionate to the caloric expenditure involved in catching the fish. On the trail back to the truck, I made a suggestion.

"I know a gas station with great tacos."

Chuck looked puzzled. I clarified.

"They also have lobster taquitos."

The Mobil station sits at the intersection of Highway 395 and Tioga

Pass, the eastern entrance to Yosemite National Park. Over gourmet gas-station food with forever views of Mono Lake basin, we planned the rest of the day. We would fish the upper Owens River and Rock Creek and end up in a rustic BLM campground under the shadow of Mount Tom.

We searched for trout. In searching we found something we weren't looking for. There are few places where guys feel comfortable talking about their struggles. Most guys I know won't have these conversations at church or men's retreats and certainly not in a small group with other couples. The better place is in the wild, where mountains put problems in perspective and lack of programs and walls gives us direct access to God. Men are made to hear God in places He created. We grow suspicious in places created by other people.

Chuck and I have very different careers but are similar in how we approach them. We work hard, too hard at times. Not because we are told to but because something inside drives us. This allows us to provide well for our families but interferes with the time we have for them. It's easy for us to get caught up in wanting to provide more and defending the extra hours it takes to provide it. Every generation of men wants more for their families than they had. So we work hard and feel justified in our work and are frustrated when the more we work, the more our families fall apart.

The setting sun cast long shadows over the Owens River valley, and light refracting behind mountains made the highest peaks appear to have halos. We found our campground in the twilight. Chuck built a fire, and I foraged in my bags for food. We forgot to buy dinner, and there was only what I usually have in my fishing bag. Beef jerky and a flask of whis-key. Chuck had a couple of granola bars. We laid what we found on a decaying picnic table. Bam, dinner.

Fire glowed warm against the cooling night, and noises of the world slumbered under descending darkness. There's comfort in campfires.

Like the feeling of a first home we can't quite remember. After the whiskey was finished and fish stories told, we talked about our families and fears and shortcomings and ways we wished we were better. Neither of us had great answers for work. Of tasks and client calls and crises there is no end. Work always wants more of your time. It always demands more attention. Chuck and I have set protective boundaries around our children, so like a mistress, work steals from our wives.

There's a long list of justifications. We're trying to get ahead. We need more money to build a room addition or take a family vacation. All have degrees of truth. They're as innocent as a first cup of coffee with the secretary.

The trip was Chuck's idea. Though he said he needed it for himself, I think he knew I needed it too. I need men like Chuck to challenge me and hold me to my promises. We all need this. We all fall short. The men we need in our lives are ones strong enough to call us on our crap and wise enough to know when we're dishing it. We sat in the light of stars and fire and made promises about how we would be better husbands. It will be hard. I will fail. But I know we'll fish again and be held accountable to our word.

They were promises made between men in search of trout, sealed with whiskey and firelight.

ENNIS
MONTANA

15

Missouri River Headwaters

287

90

Jefferson River

Three Forks

Wheat Montana (Sandwiches)

Tobacco Root Mountains

Mad Hatters (for Cowboy hats)

R.L. Winston Rod Co. HQ

15

Big Hole River

Twin Bridges

287

Norris Hot Springs

287

84

Madison River

"Biggest Skiing in America"

Gallatin River

Bozeman

Simms Fishing HQ

41

Beaverhead River

Ruby River

Star Bakery for pie

Nevada City

Ennis

Ennis Lake

Big Sky Ski Resort

Lone Mountain Ranch

Dillon
Patagonia Outlet
Sweetwater Coffee

Virginia City

Bale of Hay Saloon

MADISON RANGE

191

287

287

DOWNTOWN ENNIS

287

Ennis Sugar High Burgers & milkshakes

Ennis Pharmacy & Fountain Best Chicken fried steak around

Nearly New Shoppe (cool thrift store)

Lions Club Trout Farm for kids

WILLIAM ST.

2nd St.

3rd St.

William St.

Willie's Distillery

MAIN ST.

MAIN STREET

1st St.

2nd St.

3rd St.

Madison River Fly Fishing

The Tackle Shop

Gravel Bar

Trout Stalkers Outfitter and Fly Shop

Madison River

Wade & Cliff Lakes

87

Quake Lake

Hebgen Lake

22

The Headwaters
of Our Searching

Ennis, Montana

learned to fish from my dad, and since his death I have become obsessed with it. Every fish caught brings a little of him to life. It's hard for me to remember the look of my father, though I can remember the feeling of a fish on the end of the line and his voice coaching over my excited chatter.

"You know what to do, buddy. Not too hard. Reel it in gently."

Much of parenting is repairing that which has been broken in us. We get our kids into the things we love, or wished we had loved, and get a second chance at everything we first hoped for ourselves. Our children are the remaking of our history. I always wanted to fish more with my dad. The part of a boy's heart that longs to fish with his father is a wound nothing else can heal. Now that I'm a father, my heart continues to break knowing my boys won't experience the love of a grandfather fisherman.

Though perhaps futile, I try to heal the wound myself. This quest has led us to southwestern Montana and the Madison River Valley.

In most parts of the country when I pull into a small town in the middle of nowhere, it's pretty much what I expect. A gas station, a couple of local stores, and a greasy-spoon restaurant serving black coffee and powdered creamer. With a population of fewer than one thousand, Ennis was a surprise.

The Madison River borders the town's eastern entrance, and the western entrance features an oversized statue of a fisherman catching a trout on a fly. If life imitates art, this was a good start. A short walk up and down Main Street revealed a collection of western- and fishing-themed businesses promising the best of western Montana. My boys loved the homemade milkshakes at Yesterday's Soda Fountain, while my wife and I preferred the grown-up drinks at world-class Willie's Distillery after having great burgers at the Gravel Bar. The town has a cowboy flair; its streets are lined with trees and American flags and storefronts made of century-old wood logged from surrounding mountains. Standing on Main Street I could look east or west and see mountain ranges. The mountains and the town felt like they belonged together.

My friend Mike said his dad, Steve, was willing to be our fishing guide, and since he was an expert on the area, we took him up on it. I texted and got a short, friendly text back saying, "Call me, I'm old school." Over a quick call he gave a tip on a campground and some good places for the kids to visit. We also set up a time to fish. I'm reluctant to let people in, but there was something in his voice.

Steve arrived exactly when he said he would. He drove an older Ford truck with a cream-colored body and Big Sky Montana mud flaps. Considering the age of the truck, and the tough Montana environment, it was in surprisingly good shape. His movements were efficient, and he approached us with hand extended. He wore a flannel shirt tucked into blue jeans. His well-worn boots said he'd seen much of the world, and by the care he's given his white cowboy hat, I could tell he was a man who tended to things. There was joy in Steve's eyes, and right away I liked him. In a few minutes he had established a rapport with my boys, and even our young Australian shepherd warmed to him, though she's less wary of people in general.

The next twenty-four hours became what our family referred to as Camp Steve. It included big-game sightings and mountain treks and river floats and a lot of fly-fishing. The first session was on a creek near Steve's house. Hundreds of creeks enter the valley and share a similar story. They flow swiftly from high reaches of surrounding wilderness and, once out of the mountains and into the tall grass, assume the pace of the valley as they meander toward the Madison.

The sky stretched forever in every direction. Viewed from the Gravelly Range on the western edge of the valley, the Madison Range on the opposite side stood small against the sky. Yet mountain peaks rose higher than ten thousand feet, and the wilderness contains one of the largest wildlife corridors in North America. Gray wolves and grizzlies traverse this range all the way to Yellowstone, creating a complicated relationship with the ranchers who steward the land. Many of the ranches go back to the settling of the West by early pioneers, and under stewardship principles passed from generation to generation, the land seemed untouched.

This is an American Serengeti. In a single afternoon we spotted bald eagles, osprey, white-tailed deer, and pronghorns, the fastest land animal in the Western Hemisphere. After cresting a low ridge we saw what appeared, from a distance, to be a small brown lake. As we got nearer, the lake moved. It was a herd of elk, hundreds moving across the plain. Some of these animals we'd seen before in zoos or in traffic jams in Yellowstone National Park. But on this back road, it was just us and the land as it once was. I found myself praying it would stay that way.

Steve knew every hole on the creek, and considering the amount of fish he'd caught and released on this stretch of water, we suspected he knew every fish as well.

"There's a good hole around this bend," he said. He helped my older son tie on a caddis fly, and then they approached the hole from downstream. The hole required a pinpoint cast, and since the creek bank was thick with trees, the only way to make the cast was from knee-deep water.

"Don't worry," Steve told my son. "Your pants will dry."

The first cast was off mark but still resulted in a small strike. The second cast was perfect. My son dropped the fly softly into the strike zone, and there was an immediate flash and turbulence in the water. His line went tight and things happened in fast motion. The rod shivered. He tried to reel in some line but with equal resolve the fish pulled it out. He and the fish were working in opposites, and tension was felt both in the line and the breathless air. The trout leaped, trying to shake the fly from its mouth. It had a dark speckled top and a bright orange belly. A beautiful brook trout.

Steve stood in the creek behind my son and coached him on landing the fish. I watched my son hold the trout gently, remove the fly from its mouth, and release it back into the water. His smile was wide, almost as wide as Steve's. En route to the next hole, Steve turned to my son, who at the time was nearly twelve. Steve asked, "Have you learned to drive yet?"

"No."

"Want to?"

My son slid in behind the wheel. He couldn't reach the gas pedal when his back was touching the seat's backrest, so he sat on the front edge of the bench seat. We lurched and stopped and swerved until we hit paved road and switched back to Steve driving. My son gave a couple of driving pointers along the way.

✕

Fishing connects us to something bigger—a search that we're all on. Our collective memories of fishing have a lot to do with fathers and grandfathers and the heroes they were. Even if they weren't, they were more so while fishing. Water magnifies a man. We are drawn to water to seek men we've lost or who never were, or the men we are trying to become. We seek trout because they live in the headwaters of our searching. They swim in higher places, and to find them we have to travel up.

Water moves like time. It began in the womb of creation when earth was void and without form. There is no beginning or end to water's flow, and when I step into the river, I step into something eternal. The place where I stand is always new. So as water washes over me, I become new as well. We are made by water and for the water; it carries the scent of our beginning. It's here, on a creek in western Montana, where I discover the purpose of fishing.

Casting in shadows of the wild for a brook trout or a brown or a rainbow is not about battling a fish. Fishing is a battle for our children's hearts. Like playing catch in the yard or cheering from the sidelines of a soccer field. This world will be hard for them; an enemy is always near, plotting and scheming, stationed at the edge of our defenses, seeking a weakness. Our children will be told they are not smart enough or good-looking enough. Or a million other lies we also believed when we were young. Or still believe. Eventually the thing you think of yourself, however untrue at first, becomes true. As a fatherless child I fought this battle alone and continued as an adult. I told myself that if I kept fighting the battle, my sons wouldn't have to fight so hard.

In the waters of Montana, I realized I was wrong. The battle isn't mine to fight; it's mine to surrender. Not to an enemy, but to the One who will fight for me and others who will fight with me. Friends and mentors. A man in a white hat. These people are there; I just have to let them in. I've been wrong about something else too. Father wounds can be mended. Our hearts are mended by the love poured into our children's hearts.

I can feel my heart healing as I watch Steve teach my younger son how to land a dry fly in the current. He makes a cast to the head of a small pool between the V of two riffles. The caddis sits momentarily on the water and disappears with a violent splash. My son's rod doubles over, and his arm shakes as if he's holding the smallest point of a thunderbolt. His body is tense with happiness, and he speaks in excited chatter. Steve begins to coach, speaking instruction and encouragement. He tells my son he has what it takes to catch this fish. I chime in with instruction of my own.

"You know what to do, buddy. Not too hard. Reel it in gently."

The valley has opened like a funnel to pour into the hearts of my sons this creek and the wild and the words of men who love them. This is a good day of fishing.

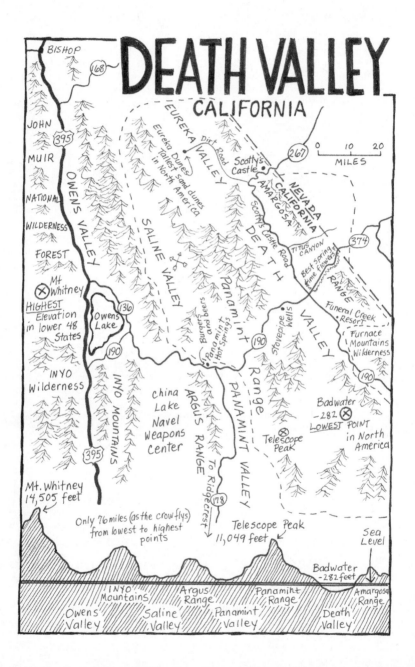

DEATH VALLEY
CALIFORNIA

BISHOP

168

395

JOHN

MUIR

NATIONAL

WILDERNESS

FOREST

OWENS VALLEY

Mt Whitney

HIGHEST Elevation in lower 48 States

Owens Lake

INYO Wilderness

136

190

INYO MOUNTAINS

395

Mt. Whitney 14,505 feet

Only 76 miles (as the crow flys) from lowest to highest points

EUREKA VALLEY

Eureka Dunes Tallest sand dunes in North America

Dirt Road

Scotty's Castle

267

0   10   20
MILES

NEVADA
CALIFORNIA

AMARGOSA

SALINE VALLEY

Scotty's Castle Road

PANAMINT

Burgers and beers

Panamint Hot Springs

China Lake Navel Weapons Center

ARGUS RANGE

To Ridgecrest

178

Telescope Peak 11,049 feet

TITUS CANYON

Best Spring time flowers

374

DEATH

Range

VALLEY

190

Stovepipe Wells

PANAMINT VALLEY

PANAMINT Range

Telescope Peak

Funeral Creek Resort

Furnace Mountains Wilderness

190

Badwater -282
LOWEST POINT in North America

Sea Level

Badwater -282 feet

INYO Mountains
Owens Valley

Argus Range
Saline Valley

Panamint Range
Panamint Valley

Death Valley

Amargosa Range

23

After the Wildflowers Are Gone

Death Valley National Park, California

I daydream about the long roads. Ones with distance enough to stretch this life thin when things have gotten too thick with myself or my problems or ambitions. When I think of these roads, my feet get restless and my heart is set in motion. I rush to a map and look for the roads between the highways.

The road has been a space for clarity, a space to look for answers or to find better questions. It can sometimes be an escape, but mostly it's a search for clues and signs. It's change of perspective.

The first sign I paid attention to on this road trip made me think I should have prepared better—or at least brought more water. "Entering Death Valley." I assumed it was literal.

I first heard about Death Valley more than two decades ago. I was exploring California's eastern deserts and mountains with my friend Brady, when he pointed to a range of snow-covered mountains and a mysterious road winding around a dry lake bed that held rusted remnants of a once-booming salt plant. Those were the long days of youth when every dirt road beckoned possibility and could be traveled without consequence of time.

On that trip, Brady and I snowboarded and fished. When fishing slowed we lassoed cattle with remnants of oil-stained rope from the bed of his truck. We slept wherever the day ended. We've remained close through the years, and his judgment is as sound as his character. He has spent a lot of time in the desert. He recently called from Death Valley to tell me a super bloom was on. Wildflowers carpeted the valley, and if I hurried I could catch it.

The super bloom is a fleeting moment in the desert when the barren floor is quilted with wildflowers. Several elements have to line up perfectly for a super bloom to occur. The rains need to begin in the fall and penetrate deep into the desert floor to activate dormant seeds. When seeds begin to germinate, the rains must come gently and consistently. Too much and the desert floods. Too little and seeds die of thirst. The ground needs to warm slowly, cooled by cloud cover and soft rains of winter. When green shoots appear, winds must be mild and forgiving so plants can dance in the safe grace of sunlight. The odds of all this happening in the same growing season mean seeing the bloom is a rare event. One worth seeking.

The drive was long and lonesome. In Panamint Valley, the only other soul I saw was in the cockpit of a fighter jet doing maneuvers over the desert. I waved and he acknowledged with a tip of his wings. Cresting a summit looking into Death Valley I expected a basin of yellow and orange, an inland sea of color. But the land was barren. I had missed the bloom.

I've always struggled with feeling I missed opportunities. That maybe if I had strived a little harder or was in the right place at the right time, I could have been more successful and made more money. I could have been celebrated in my calling. I entered Death Valley at a point in life when the roads ahead appeared shorter than the ones behind. The chances of a super bloom in my life were unrealistic, and I wondered what beauty was left after the wildflowers were gone.

There's a refuge on the western edge of Death Valley built around a natural spring. The man-made oasis includes a gas station, a restaurant, and a bar that serves more than one hundred types of beer. Panamint Springs is rustic and off the grid and has an Old West feel to it, possibly because it was founded by a runaway cousin of Buffalo Bill Cody. I grabbed a burger and beer and sat next to a couple who have been coming here every spring for more than twenty years. They said on every visit they discover a new scar in the earth and in it find unexpected beauty. Though that's not the only reason they come.

"It resets our souls."

They could tell I was interested.

"We come here to be reminded how small we are. This place helps us maintain perspective."

I told them I came for the super bloom and how disappointed I was to have missed it. They let me know that "the wildflowers are only a small part of the beauty."

They told me Death Valley National Park is a series of valleys: Panamint Valley, Death Valley, Saline Valley, and Eureka Valley. Separating the valleys are mountain ranges that hide seldom-explored mines and ghost towns and living towns, such as Darwin, that will make you think you saw ghosts.

They suggested I visit Titus Canyon in the northeast corner of the park. It winds through a deep scar in the Grapevine Mountains. It's a narrow one-way road snaking through limestone walls gray with age. There is no water present, but water has left its mark. As have the people of previous cultures who left hints of their history with petroglyphs. Walls rise vertically hundreds of feet above a narrow floor that always is in shadow.

South of Titus Canyon, Badwater Basin is a salt flat that descends to the lowest elevation in North America, at 279 feet below sea level. Yet it's only eighty-five miles from the highest point in the contiguous United States. In high-rain years the basin fills and the white salt-pan is covered with thin sheets of mirrored water. When the wind blows just right, it smells of ocean.

The beauty of Death Valley is in its wounds. Mountains are bald with every wrinkle shown and every scar exposed. In every way the land has been stripped bare. There are no trees. There is no water. The attraction is the honesty.

I called Brady and told him I missed out on the bloom. This led to a conversation about how I was struggling with my perception of success. He asked me how the important things were going. Family. Friends. Faith. Brady has experienced every high and low in life, and he is sought after because of his entrepreneurial achievements. But his influence in my life comes from his time in the desert.

I've chased success because, I've reasoned, with success comes a platform in which to change the world. This is partially true. A platform allows opportunity to connect with lots of people, but success is a shallow change agent. For generations, people of faith have sought to change the world. To do this we've led with our strengths. Yet the world continues much the same, indifferent to our efforts. Our strength will not win the hearts of the world, because hearts are moved by beauty. The world will see our beauty only when we are willing to reveal our scars.

YOSEMITE NATIONAL PARK
and Surrounding Area

Hetch Hetchy Reservoir

Tuolumne River

Lee Vining

120

120

Road closed in winter

Tuolumne Meadows

120

Yosemite Village

MERCED RIVER

Glacier Pt.

Tunnel View

Yosemite National Park Border

__Oakhurst__
- Branches Books is a must!
- South Gate Brewery for beers & good food
- Cool Beans (coffee)
- Queen's Inn wine bar & winery

Historic Wawona Hotel

140

41

Sugar Pine Narrow Gauge Railroad

Beasore Meadows

Jones General Store

Several chapters of My Best Friend's Funeral are about this area

Mammoth Pool Reservoir

49

Oakhurst

Bass Lake

The Forks for burgers & lake view

Ice cream & boat watching at the South Fork Pines Marina

To China Peak Snow resort

Coursegold

North Fork

San Joaquin River

168

La Cabana Mexican Food

Slim's Koffee Shak

Shaver Lake

0   5   10
MILES

41

Fresno

Auberry

- Shaver Lake Pizza
- Bob's Blue Sky Cafe

24

A Sideways Glance at Heaven

Yosemite National Park, California

Rog, this is the end."

"No, Grandpa. It can't be."

It's too soon. I want life to return to his failing body. I want the cancer to go away. I want more time.

"Roger. Buddy. You're going to have to accept this."

I can't. I try. I can't.

His eyes closed and he drifted off. I watched his chest to make sure he was still breathing. It was my turn to watch, to wait for the ringing of the bell when he needed something. I loved the sound of the bell. It meant Grandpa was awake one more time.

You can hold someone's hand until his last breath, knowing that it is coming. And when the breathing stops and the bed sheet goes still and you know exactly what is happening, it will feel too soon. For the space between here and hereafter is eternal, as our love is meant to be. Anything shorter feels too soon.

Grandpa was lying on a hospital bed that was set up in his living room. The house was quiet and dark. I looked over lights of Ventura. The twinkling was a reminder of how the world goes on, indifferent. Grandpa needed rest, so I disappeared into his garage. There were two old patio chairs on a small rug. I sat in the same one I always did and stared at the motorcycles.

Grandpa taught me how to ride in mountains behind the cabin. He called the cabin his other home, but the way he talked about it led me to believe he meant the mountains surrounding the cabin. He referred to them as "our mountains." The cabin was nestled on Bass Lake, outside the southern entry to Yosemite National Park. The mountains behind the cabin are surrounded by three great wilderness areas: the Greater Yosemite Wilderness, the Ansel Adams Wilderness, and the John Muir Wilderness. They connect to several others, creating one of the longest continuous wilderness areas in the United States. It's the spine of California, filled with countless rivers and lakes and glaciers providing life to the rest of the state in the form of water. A short distance from the cabin, a series of mountain byways and dirt roads and trails lead into the expanse.

I stared at the trickle charger attached to the battery of Grandpa's BMW dual sport motorcycle. The battery had long been dead, and hooking up the charger was a mark of false hope. My mind drifted.

"Hey, Rog. Let's take a ride through our mountains."

From the cabin we rode south to North Fork, the exact center of the state, then east into the wilderness. The road ascended almost forever until we scraped the bottom of the sky. Views along the high ridge led our eyes past the peaks and bald granite domes guarding remote wilds of the San Joaquin River. I could see into all three wilderness areas and maybe beyond. For the entire morning we saw no one else.

Mountaintops give vision to life but cannot sustain it. Life is lived in the valleys, so we descended. We ordered coffee in a wood-clad general store at Mammoth Pool Reservoir. Grandpa asked if I wanted to head back home or keep going. If we decided to head back, we could get to the cabin by lunch. If we kept going it would be hours of hard riding. The payoff, though, would be ancient trees and crystal-clear waters and meadows and mountains and a wide-open road.

"Let's keep going."

I learned to ride by following Grandpa into the wilderness. In the beginning I rode in front of him sitting on his motorcycle. As I grew I started sitting behind him with my arms wrapped around his chest. As I held on, I learned how it felt to take the bike into a corner. The slowing into the curve. The lean. The acceleration out of it. When I was big enough to ride on my own, he made me learn hand signals so we could communicate while I followed on my motorcycle. He signaled when to slow or when to turn or when there was gravel in the road. Eventually I no longer needed hand signals and learned by watching. If he rode the crown into a turn, I knew it would be shallow and fast. If he rode lower, closer to the shoulder, I knew it was a blind curve.

Our ride from the general store at Mammoth Pool Reservoir looped over another summit and into high mountain meadows of tall grasses and wild purple lupines. On the edge of the largest meadow sat the Jones Store. It had been there for more than one hundred years, and the age showed in the faded red siding, rusted tin roof, and been-here-until-they-became-antiques, such as the hand-pumped gravity-fed gas pump. We celebrated the ride with homemade pie shared in the shade of trees much older than the store. We talked late into the afternoon about faith and family and the open road. On the last leg of our ride that day, Grandpa pulled to the shoulder and waved me to him.

"Hey, buddy. Why don't you lead the rest of the way home?"

I found Grandpa's riding jacket in the garage. I tried it on and it fit. I looked through the pictures he left on his workbench. It was like visiting his favorite memories. The family rafting down the Snake River. The family at the cabin. Pictures of my dad. I came across an old shot of Grandpa and me in riding gear in the cabin's garage. We were heading for a ride through the tunnel and into The Park.

The Wawona Tunnel is the longest highway tunnel in California, carved from solid granite bedrock. Whenever I entered it I held my breath. It was a long, straight darkness through the mountain with only a hope of light at the end. On a bend before entering it, we'd get a glimpse of what's on the other side. It was a sideways glance, enough to sense a glory beyond measure, but no chance to take it in. The only way to experience the glory is to get there through the darkness. The moment I entered I was chasing the light.

The first view of Yosemite after passing through the tunnel is something of a fantasy. A reflection of heaven with blinding light in undimmed glory. I passed through the halo and my eyes adjusted. I found that the beauty could not be registered by sight alone. Every best thing in the natural world is held in this valley. The sky is outlined by granite, known as Half Dome, El Capitan, and Glacier Point. These legends conjure images even for those who never have experienced their majesty. In the distance, mountains stack upon mountains with continuous views of granite and green broken only by glaciers held in fissures of stone. Above the valley stand peaks and ridges of arched rock lined with evergreens. Any place a seed could take root, a tree had grown. In places they cascaded from ridges to valley and pooled like water—level, serene, and still.

In every dip of granite, water spilled. Where the wind caught it, water-darkened stone contrasted against lacy patterns of waterfalls. During snowmelt, waterfalls tumbled in torrents and trickles, and since it's hard to imagine a higher source of water, I was left to assume the waterfalls came from headwaters of heaven. It was the only way to make sense of the beauty. Everything in the valley pointed up.

After the tunnel, the road lowered us gently to the valley floor. This was a more human scale. More understood. It felt more natural to plant feet into earth and look up. It's the difference between what we're created from and what we're created for.

From there the highway became a one-way road circling the valley. Our first stop was Bridalveil Fall, a thin ribbon of water leaping fearlessly into a 620-foot-deep void where it disappeared into mist. The wind carried the water, and even from a distance we were refreshed. The Native Americans believed inhaling the mist would improve one's chance of marriage, but Grandpa was too old and I was too young to care much about that.

Deeper the road carried us. Around a river bend and into a meadow where light came late to the valley floor. The grasses bent with a burden of light, and the meadow was fenced with autumn oaks. Where the river touched the meadow, it was lined with cottonwoods so filled with sun they appeared as pure flame. Yellow and red and gold. Leaves so heavy with beauty they could no longer hang from limbs. They fell. And fell. And fell. In descent they joined with others. A ballet of leaves and light danced to a soft melody of autumnal winds.

The leaves came to rest on the road, and the road glowed. We rode under a canopy of cottonwood and oak through a coolness greater than any warmth offered by our leather. Grandpa was in front, surrounded by diffused light. His tires brought leaves to life where they had been lying along the road. Again they twirled and danced in the swirls of motorcycle wind. I entered a world brought to life by my grandfather, and as I rhythmically leaned my bike into a left-hand turn and again to the right, I was dancing too. Beyond asphalt and engine, meadow and oak, I was riding the light.

Every road trip has an end. The quality of ending is a reflection of choices made along the way. Our destination was the grand Ahwahnee Hotel, a historic structure built of carved stone and rough-hewn timber. It rose from manicured grounds as a reflection of its surroundings. Sturdy and timeless, as if it were built in the age of kings. Presidents and dignitaries had walked the halls, but in that moment none compared to my grandpa. We warmed ourselves by fireplaces large enough to deter chill in the deep snows of winter. Grandpa told me I rode well.

We ordered coffee and sat in wooden furniture at the edge of the grass where we looked upon pines and granite.

"It's the best cappuccino in The Park," he told me. After a moment of reflection, he added to his thought. "Or maybe, it's the view."

The Merced River lay just beyond the hotel grounds. From its headwaters it cascaded nearly one thousand feet down Nevada and Vernal Falls. Once it reached the valley floor, it collected itself, slowing through forests and meadows. It unwound languidly, in places nearly bending back upon itself, as if the water too wanted to take in the view.

As I stood in Grandpa's garage holding old photos, I didn't notice when the tears started. They flooded like memories. I wanted to ask Grandpa if he remembered that ride or other rides. I wanted to ask where the other roads led, but we were beyond the time for questions. I took off his jacket and wiped my eyes and walked into the house. The bell was ringing.

YOSEMITE
NATIONAL PARK

El Capitan

Northside Drive

Southside Drive

← TO HWY 140   El Portal Road   MERCED RIVER

TUNNEL VIEW

0   ½   1 mile

The Long Lingering of Autumn

Yosemite National Park, California

In Yosemite, winter snow falls in perfect silence. The valley is in thought. The only sounds are soft crunching of snow and wind hushed by pines.

In spring, life looks forward. It's a deluge of wildflowers and water, full of promise. Summer is a chaos of cars and tour buses and people posting pictures of trails they never intend to hike, and the frenzy of summer activity doesn't slow until the first winds of autumn. But in winter, life looks back. Water is frozen for a moment and does not move. It can be examined, slowly. Smoke rises from chimneys of the Ahwahnee, and scents of burned oak mingle with descending snowflakes.

This is the slow language of our memories. They can be followed as they fall, quivering in time. At winter's speed, memories make sense—both the beautiful and the ugly. Soon they will gather with all memories, and they will fall with the snow, and the brokenness of this world will be covered in white.

Grandpa was lying motionless. The bell was placed on a folding tray that also held a small city of amber-colored pill containers. They were organized with largest containers in the back so all the labels could be read. On the white label of the morphine-pill container, in Grandpa's broken handwriting, were the words *feel good*.

"Grandpa, you call these your 'feel good' pills?"

"Well, that's what they do."

He chuckled as we went through our routine of adjusting pillows and sheets and taking pills. I'd asked him about some of the things he'd miss most. He'd been silent on the subject until now.

"I'll miss watching the great-grandkids grow. And the family. And sitting on the deck of the cabin when the sun rises over our mountains."

Grandpa started going to Bass Lake in the fifties. He and Grandma would go with church groups and camp along the shore, yelling, "Elmer!" They yelled through the night just to hear someone yell it back. Over a half century Grandpa moved from tents to trailer and from trailer to cabin, until he finally secured the cabin of his dreams. I picture him on the end of the deck looking out. The early morning is still and smells of pine trees and coffee. The world is silent except for occasional sounds of fish jumping. Grandpa sits as still as Goat Mountain. The sun has yet to rise over the pines, and the water is motionless with patches of mist. Between the patches, water reflects the light pink of the sky.

The water is down and the lake is narrow, maybe a quarter of a mile across at the cabin. But it's long, and Grandpa is staring the length of it. Halfway down the lake, the sheriff tower is shaped like a large Tootsie Pop stuck into the ground. It sits on a peninsula that turns into an island when the water is high. In the distance, the lake disappears into the mist, and it's hard to see a separation between water and sky.

Mirrored in still waters are the surrounding ponderosa pines standing more than two hundred feet above the lake. Rising above the pines are layers of mountains, each ridge rising higher in successive patterns. The mountains and trees and lake remain the same, yet every morning the sight is different. We bring the morning our thoughts and plans and worries, and it brings us stillness and beauty. Together we turn it into day.

Every morning that I have awakened at the cabin, I've found Grandpa in his favorite spot at the end of the deck. He sits there drinking coffee. I've come to know this view only with him in it.

The deck vibrates with my walking, and Grandpa knows it's me without turning to look.

"Morning, buddy."

I sit for a while and we both are silent.

"Want to go for a ride?"

"Yes. Where are we going?"

"Let's take the old road and follow the river into The Park."

Our helmets sat display-like on the workbench in the garage, and our leathers were hanging in a closet with a couple of shop brooms. The leathers were aged with wind and time. We suited up while motorcycle engines warmed. He'd be riding the BMW dual sport 1100 while I rode the eighties-era BMW 750 road bike.

Mornings on motorcycles were brutally cold in the mountains. We wore layers, knowing that warm clothing was no match for the cold. At best we could dull it. But it didn't matter; we rode. He gave me directions on the roads we'd ride, but it wasn't necessary. His maps had long been printed on my heart. We pulled out of the garage and down the drive. The cabin receded into the distance until I could no longer see Grandma's silhouette in the window.

This was his favorite ride, from the cabin through Yosemite National Park, with cappuccinos at the Ahwahnee. It was my favorite too.

Since he was more awake than usual, I indulged Grandpa in a ride through memories.

"Do you remember our motorcycle rides into The Park?" There was his grin, the one that recalled or began some mischief.

"Those were good times."

"Yes, they were. Except when we got to the tunnel. Every time we got there, you would ride so fast I couldn't keep up."

Grandpa laughed quietly. Contentedly. It was a diminished echo of his once-deep laughter. Like trying to call for someone over too much wind. I held his hand, and for the first time my hand felt warmer than his.

"Rog, I'm there."

"Where, Grandpa? Where are you?"

His eyes closed.

"I'm there."

"Where, Grandpa? I'm sitting right here with you."

His words were breathless, hanging on crevices of dried lips.

"It's beautiful, Rog. Beautiful."

I'm trying hard to hold back tears. To not bring my burden to Grandpa. For once in my life to be the strong one, and he knows.

"It's okay, Rog. Everything will be okay."

My voice is broken.

"What's it like, Grandpa?"

He smiles.

"It's peace."

He trailed off into distant sleep. I never heard the bell again.

When the coroner came they wheeled him out of the house. A lifetime of photos looked on from hallway walls. Marriage. Kids. Grandkids in grade school. Grandkids getting married. Great-grandkids. Family vacations. The cabin. Photos of favorite memories and the people he loved watching him roll past under thin sheets.

I went back to the garage to hide between the motorcycles. Grandpa was my gravity, and I suddenly felt untethered, afloat in a world I struggled to understand. I still had so many questions. I tried to steady myself on the motorcycle, but I couldn't. I could not contain the shaking and heaving and shallow breaths followed by deep groans. I could not control my traitorous eyes or trembling hands.

I held a picture of Grandpa but could not see it. It floated in trembled blur. There was no stopping the flow. We grieve at the depth of our love.

Death is a journey with a map I never read. I knew the destination. I feared it. I once again learned by following Grandpa, riding behind into his last days. Death is a road best ridden with no regrets and with relationships restored. With an understanding of who our God is and a peace that we know Him.

Grandpa went with a restless tapping of his feet and a compass tested in truth, pointed to the last uncharted wilderness. The map to our final peace is a redeemed life, well lived. When it is that, death will come in love, not fear. Grandpa's weary body had come to rest, yet his soul began another ride. Curled between the motorcycles, I imagined riding with him as far as I could.

A short distance from the cabin we enter The Park. We've made a few turns and gained speed on a straightaway, limbering the muscles of the bikes. To get to our destination in the Yosemite Valley floor requires a long, steady ascent. Over peaks and ridges and rivers, through sequoias and ponderosa pines, with intimate scenes of water tumbling and tangling upon itself and mountaintops breaking through morning haze, silhouettes of distant peaks curated higher and higher in deeper shades of blue.

Highway 41 is empty in late fall, and we have the roads and wilder-

ness to ourselves. We get accustomed to our new surroundings, then find our legs and our speed. Fast enough to feel the chill of shaded pines through worn leathers. Relaxed enough to capture fleeting images in the slow-motion lenses of passing memory. Light through the trees creates a rhythm of black-and-white keys on the asphalt. We play the notes with our motorcycles, speeding and slowing through crescendos of curves and vistas as we float through songs of Yosemite.

We approach the Wawona Tunnel, and I know from previous passages that after miles of winding limitations, Grandpa is anxious to pick up speed. He's in complete control of his motorcycle, as if it were an extension of himself. He is both in the moment and above it. His head lowers and he releases the clutch. The bike lurches and he becomes a blur. An essence of himself somehow bigger. There is nothing in the tunnel but darkness and uncertainty. Yet he gains speed. He cocks his head slightly to see me in his mirror, to make sure I'm safe. Then he lowers his head and shifts into another gear and disappears alone into the darkness.

He's gone. I can't go after him.

✕

Some of my best days were spent riding with Grandpa. We become who we are through imitation. Life is unpredictable. The best indicator of how things might be for us is a careful study of those we follow. I followed Grandpa's lead and learned to be a man by copying how he rode. I had an insatiable appetite for my grandfather and constantly asked to be with him. To ride. To drive. To sit and drink coffee. He made time for me. Grandpa let me ride with him as far as I could, to the threshold of heaven. But every ride comes to an end. At the end of his, he was met by Jesus, who took him the rest of the way home. I can no longer see him with my eyes. But in my heart I know he still rides. The ride into The Park was Grandpa's favorite. This next ride will be even greater.

He races from the tunnel into pure light of heaven. It emanates from every created thing. From the trees and the tall shrubs and the meadows and from his own body. The world before the Fall was carved by light. It shines again in the long days of resurrection, bright as the moment you step from shadow.

The road follows the river. It winds higher and deeper through the valley and into the source of all light. It's the road home. Grandpa will rise along watersheds and ridges of a restored earth with vistas into the unfiltered beauty of creation. When beauty overtakes him, the road will guide him gently down into eternal shade of oaks and evergreens, where he'll meet with scents of sage after a soft rain. The trees are heavy with light, and the leaves let go. They glow in reflected grace, and the world is aflutter. Leaves fall and dance and blanket the earth, paving the streets in gold. The road opens up. He downshifts and leans and turns, sweeping perfectly into the long lingering of autumn.

Yosemite has long been a spiritual place. It's impossible to gaze upon the granite cliffs, waterfalls, and forests and not be stirred. The Native Americans who took the time to lean into the stirring concluded there was something bigger at work. On every scale, the surroundings are larger than life. Cliffs stand tall enough to block the sun and water falls eternal. Yet the valley floor lives at a human scale. The surrounding giants stand guard, to protect. Even now, when I come out of the Wawona Tunnel and into the light of the valley, I can feel something at work. I look up and lean into the stirring. When I return through the passage, out of the valley and toward home, I carry the gift of Yosemite with me. Healing. Hope. Grace. It is a sideways glance into glories of heaven.

FLY
HATCH

Emerger   Dry Fly

Fly-fishing flies
are imitations of the
natural aquatic fly life cycle

Nymph

FLY-FISHING GEAR
HERE'S WHAT I USE*

On My Lanyard
- Fly Box
- Fly Floatant
- Clippers
- Forceps
- Split shot weights
- Thingamabobber
- Extra leaders and tippet
- Fly drying patch

Don't forget
sunscreen
& lip balm

Fly Rods & Reels
- Orvis
- R.L.Winston
- Jefferson Rod Co.

Tenkara Rods
- Causwell
- Patagonia
Simple compact rods
that telescope to
full length

Clothing & accessories
- Salt & Steel

LUCKY FLY-FISHING SHIRT
- Patagonia Sun Stretch shirt with side zipper chest pockets

WADERS
- Simms G3 guide stockingfoot
- Patagonia Gunnison Gorge Wading pants

YETI

Wood and
Rubber Net

Wading boots

Fishing Bag

Sons of Trade
Satellite Sling

✱ It's taken me 20 years to accumulate this gear.
You can get started with nothing more than a Tenkara Rod

26

The Secrets of Fishing Holes

Undisclosed Location

There aren't many secret fishing holes left, particularly in California. I have a few, and though I'm sure they're no secret I've never seen anyone else fishing them.

I discovered one of my favorites on the last day of fishing season. The known holes were packed, and I was searching for solitude. It was late into fall, and at this higher elevation trees had lost their leaves, leaving patches of brown among the evergreens. But along this creek the colors held. They blazed in angled sunlight until afternoon winds snatched the last bits of color from cottonwoods, delivering leaves softly to the water below. Red and gold and yellow, like tiny rafts in the current. Below the leaves swam wild trout.

Getting to this section of the creek required navigating a rutted dirt road and a short hike down a steep ravine. Yet for difficulty of access, it was not remote. It was in the shadow of the same peaks that shaded better-known fishing holes. I'm usually in a rush to get to the water, but on this day things were moving in slow motion. Someone I loved had just died. Death is not done well in our culture; the expectation is always to move on. I was finding this hard to do. When words of counselors and clergy fall short, sometimes fishing helps. There's a clearer voice that echoes through the mountains.

At its widest point the creek was little bigger than a one-way street and never more than waist deep. The brush grew thick along the banks and shaded the edges. Openings to the sky were narrower than the creek, but through them the sun shone strong and reflected from the water's surface, making the gold in the trees glow from below. The creek could be fished only from the middle. With no room for back casts, I would have to improvise with low, side-arm casting, holding twenty feet of line only inches above the water's surface. In rivers below autumn canyons of cottonwoods, the only sounds are moving water, and only the highest peaks can be seen. The world is edited and made simple. My thoughts were reduced to fish and which fly would make a wild trout rise.

Death is a knot at the end of a fly line. It cannot be undone, yet it connects us with something bigger. A hope. I tie a fly on the line. I'm fishing for that part of me that has gone with the one I loved. I've come to realize much of mourning is trying to recapture treasures buried with our loved ones. Not things, but time spent, moments accumulated. It is hard and beautiful, filled with sorrow and joy. When someone we love dies, these moments are turned into something more perfect. I mourn for those moments, and I wonder if I ever can be whole once they are gone.

I recall experiences with my grandfather in time with a four-count rhythm and a fly line looping through shadows upon water. On the surface all that has passed is in motion. The river is clearing its own mind, removing dying leaves of fall and preparing for a new season. Below death there is life. Caddis and mayflies and Blue Winged Olives lay eggs in the water. The eggs later will emerge and hatch as aquatic flies that nourish wild trout. I cast my fly delicately between fallen leaves. It drifts for a moment and disappears in a splash.

The line goes tight and erratic. My fly rod pulses with energy, and every movement of the fish registers through the rod and into my palm. The fish and I are inextricably connected. Through a knot holding an artificial fly, now hooked in the mouth of a wild trout, I become part of the river and part of the season and part of the mountains and part of the water.

The trout fights with all the instincts of its wildness. The tip of my rod jerks toward fallen branches along the creek bank. I try to lead it another direction. The rod jerks left, then right, the fish fighting as one twice its size. I carefully reel in line, keeping steady pressure but not so much that I might break the tippet. Near my boots the orange dots along the trout's side shine like little suns. The fish makes one last attempt, then goes quiet. With wetted hands I cradle the fish and carefully remove the fly. This trout is small, no more than eight or nine inches in length. However, the life in it is bigger. It connects me more intimately with this world. I release the trout, and it goes on with its search for food.

Though wounds of loss never will heal fully, I always leave the water more whole. As I make new memories, I am remaking the part of me that was lost with my grandfather's death. I am restitching myself with a beauty whose purpose is not to heal but to help complete. I've brought many problems to this stretch of water over the years. Sometimes I catch fish; sometimes I don't. But in search of trout, I always find what I need. How this fishing hole does this I may never know. This is its secret.

GLACIER
NATIONAL PARK
& Surrounding Area

LOWER St. Mary Lake

POLEBRIDGE
the best destination
bakery in America

Camas Road

St. Mary Lake

Going to the Sun Road

WHITEFISH RANGE

Flathead River

LAKE McDONALD

Whitefish Lake

WEST GLACIER

Two Medicine Lake

WHITEFISH

Middle Fork Flathead River

EAST GLACIER

19

Whitefish
• Great Northern Brewing Co.
• Whitefish Mountain Ski Resort
• Red Caboose frozen yogurt
for coffee & Second Street pizza

93

FLATHEAD RANGE

2

Backslope Brewing Co.

BOB MARSHALL WILDERNESS

2

KALISPELL
• De Soto Grill & B.B.Q
• Colter Coffee
• Sweet Peaks Ice Cream

93

SWAN RANGE

Hungry Horse Reservoir

0   10   20   30
MILES

35

BIG FORK

83

Flathead Lake Lodge

Bigfork
• "Wild Mile" Whitewater festival
• Flathead Lake Brewing Co.
• Garden Bar for burgers & live music
• Galleries and shopping

South Fork Flathead River

SWAN LAKE

Flathead Lake

Wild Horse Island

MISSION RANGE

SWAN RIVER RANGE

93

Finley Point

35

Polson

Fishing & watersports / paddle boarding on Flathead Lake

93

Stop at a local cherry stand on eastside of lake

Hike to Holland Falls
Canoe or paddle board at Holland Lake

Lakeside camping or Holland Lake Lodge

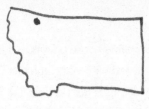

27

Echoes of God

Glacier National Park, Montana

It's hard for me to teach my boys the things I have not mastered. We tend to teach below our level of understanding so we can be confident in the teaching.

What my boys want, what all boys want, is to know how to be a man and what the world will be like once they become one. They want to know what they are capable of, how far they can push things. Though they don't know how to say it, they want to know how to abandon the fear that keeps them from trying to achieve something great. They want to know how to believe they can become someone great. Though we don't know how to say it either, as men we still want the same things.

I'm thinking of these things as I stand on the shore of Lake McDonald in Glacier National Park. I knew I needed to come here with my family. We journeyed a great distance to sit at the foot of these mountains, gazing at reflections of glaciered peaks we could never touch. There is a purity of light surrounding these high places that cuts through the cluttered questions I've been asking. Questions about how to turn boys into men. I've consulted the maps and thought if I brought the boys here, I could show them the distant peaks of manhood, and we could climb them together.

As I look now, I realize this is not possible. I am a flawed man and a flawed father. Each peak stands as an image of perfection, and even if a better version of myself could reach one, there is no way to reach them all. The image is an illusion, slipping behind a clouded veil or disappearing when the water stirs.

Such is the problem of fatherhood. In youth, the world is full of wonder. Anything is possible. With the fading of age, we men know a different world. Unforgiving, full of danger and regret. It's best just to play it safe.

Still, we try to teach things we do not know or have lost along the way. Not math or how to kick a soccer ball. It's more. We are trying to teach our sons they can do anything they set their will to. That if they truly believe, they can achieve more than we have. We try to teach them how to become the men we have yet to become. But I can no more teach my boys these things than I can teach them how to play violin in a symphony or how to skin a buffalo. I can only take them to the edge of a lake in this northern territory and with no more than the compass of learned character, point and pray.

Like the psalmist, I looked to the mountains and asked where my help would come from. From this shoreline the peaks tower in every direction, the highest summits distinguished by glaciers that from a distance look like long white beards. They appear as a gathering of wise men who know of this age and the ages before. For they were there when God first spoke to creation and separated heaven from earth. And they carry with them a memory of heaven, made available for anyone willing to stand at the water's edge and look up.

I now stand with my boys in the water, hoping that memories of mountains will do the thing I am not wise enough, nor strong enough, to do. To shape them into men.

There is a higher purpose of adventure. An adventure simultaneously reveals who we are capable of becoming and nudges us in that direction. Even more, an adventure does the same for our children. Before they are plagued with doubts about what they can't do, a good adventure shows them what they *can*. And the more they hike the mountain, or cross the river, or stare at the stars, the more they will ask the bigger questions and believe in the bigger version of themselves. On the playground they wonder if they have the superpowers to overcome their fears; a good adventure will prove to them that they do.

On this road trip, our adventures begin with a drive on Going-to-the-Sun Road and end with a half-day float down the north fork of the Flathead River. The Blackfeet Indians first traveled the pass over the mountains on their vision quests, hoping for wisdom from their god. As time passes, this quest remains the same, and the road unveils itself as a long ascent into heaven, each bend revealing a deeper and higher view into the creation of earth. I hope these views will stir something in the souls of my boys, leading them to ask the questions even bigger than these mountains.

Instead, they mostly ask, "Do we have any snacks?" And "Can I pee on that snow?"

But when we stop at a mountain pass or along a bend in the river, they will for a moment look up and pause, and I can see in their eyes something is changing. It is one small etch of the glacier shaping them. Then they quickly look away. There is a grace that allows us to take in only as much beauty as we can handle. Its entire glory may kill us.

Like a boy, a man can be shaped only by something bigger or harder than he is. It is the constant colliding of our wills against our limitations, or against our fears, or our fathers, or the fathers we are trying to become. These are the glaciers that chip away at us, carving the softer earth until only the mountain of manhood remains. This process most notably begins at adolescence—seen in battles of wit and wills over video games and vegetables on a dinner plate and bedtime hours. It continues until our death. Though the battlegrounds will change, the battle remains the same. The expediency of wants and leisure against the choices we know to be better. The couch over running shoes. Lust for other women over our wives. Work over our kids. It's easy to believe that being a man is watching the game after a long Monday in the office. But beer and football no more make a man than a bucket of water makes an ocean.

Some of these lessons can be taught only with time. Yet some can be taught in the higher and wilder places of this earth. When a boy fords a stream half as deep as he is tall, a pocket of fear is replaced with courage. When a boy asks his father which knot will hold, he learns there is wisdom that will provide a fish. And when, with cut shins and bruised knees, a boy seeks his mother, he learns of a love greater than the suffering of this world. This is why mountains matter and why men have been seeking their wisdom since Moses first climbed one to try to see God.

My boys are waist deep in the north fork of the Flathead River. One is searching for trout and the other for a toad. I am searching for something that until now I believed was beyond reach. I am looking to the mountains for wisdom in how to be a father and how to raise my sons in a world that increasingly believes fathers no longer matter. I am looking to the Maker of these mountains to stand in the gap of what I have to offer my boys and what I want for them. I am seeking God, looking to the mountains and asking where my help will come from.

His words are written in the wind and along the riffles and under the stones my boys are turning in their river search. I can see His handwriting all around me. It's a poem penned in wildflowers and the quaking of aspen leaves. The mountain peaks have continued to echo the voice of God since He first called them into place. Those echoes will tell my boys that they have what it takes to become men. Then the sound will bounce off my sons and tell me the same.

In the shadows of these great mountains and the light reflected from rivers that run through them, the answers come in sounds of wind and water cut by rock, and in the silence greater than it all. For there is an ancient language spoken under the glaciers of Montana, only to be heard in these higher places. Like Moses, in this light I have experienced something beyond all description. I will come down from these mountains as someone who has seen the face of God.

WASHINGTON
SAN JUAN ISLANDS

CANADA
USA WASHINGTON
CANADA
USA

ORCAS ISLAND

San Juan Island

LOPEZ ISLAND

5
To Seattle

EAST SOUND
• Darvill's Book Store
• Teezer's Coffee & cookies
• Mijitas Mexican Kitchen
• Lower Tavern
• Shearwater Kayak Adventures
• Kathryn Taylor Chocolates

ORCAS ISLAND

0 1 2
MILES

Waldron Island

Sunset at West Beach

Amazing Skate Park

East Sound

Mount Constitution highest point in San Juan Islands

Inn at Ship Bay

Moran State Park

ORCAS ROAD

East Sound

Mountain Lake

Deer Harbor Road

West Sound

West Sound

Cascade Lake

Doe Bay

Rosario Resort

Orcas Island Eclipse Charters Whale Watching

Olga

Cliff Jumping at Cascade Lake

Deer Harbor

Orcas Hotel Cafe Ferry Landing

Deer Harbor Inn & Restaurant Call Ryan Carpenter and he'll tell you good stories over an epic dinner

Coffee or breakfast before the ferry

Deep November

San Juan Islands, Washington

I was nervous the ferry would tip. Having rounded the leeward corner of the island, we were in open water where the brunt of gale-force winds slammed the ferry broadside. The boat listed to starboard. Metal creaked. The downward bow, pushed by the gale toward the water, was only a few feet above the ocean's surface. Water was splashing into the ferry. But no one seemed concerned. Crewmen stared stoically out over the whitecaps. Passengers slept or carefully drank coffee.

I made contingency plans. I located several life preservers that I could fashion into a raft. From having watched *Titanic,* I knew that when the ship sinks it will take us all under for a bit before we pop back to the surface. I told my wife to stay calm. As long as we had a plan everything would be fine. When she popped up from the water after the ferry sank, I explained, she just needed to listen for my voice. I'd find her and rescue her. She rolled her eyes and asked what time our flight was.

We spent the weekend on Orcas Island celebrating my wife's fortieth birthday. We had been together half her life, long enough for her to know my mind needs to work out scenarios and test them for a reaction. I'm not a marriage expert, but I've learned something about myself that has helped our relationship stay strong. I need our marriage to be part of a bigger adventure. One where she needs to be rescued or wooed or taken to a nice cantina for tacos. (Though in real life she usually rescues me.)

I get bored easily and suffocate with too much of the same thing. Early in our marriage I escaped in books. I read every life-planning and business book I could find, favoring ones that promised a few steps or days to achieve the life I dreamed of. I would spend a weekend reading and envisioning and writing down the revelations. Then Monday hit and I was back into a routine and bored again. I bought more books, but the problem is when you're hungry, a picture of a hamburger will never satisfy. Then I realized that for the cost of a life-planning session or couples retreat, or even a pile of marriage books, I could take my wife on a romantic weekend trip. There I got the real hamburger.

Orcas rises from the Salish Sea; it is the highest of the San Juan Islands and by distance is nearly as close to Canada as the United States. My wife and I arrived by planes and cars and boats and ended up about as far from home as we could be and remain along the West Coast. Our phones didn't work.

The island is shaped like a horseshoe, with its main village set in the innermost bend. We walked holding hands along vintage Main Street. The sun, hung low on its early winter arc, cast flattering light on shingled cottages snuggled deep in the bay of the East Sound. Life is busy, and love struggles at high speeds. If it doesn't have time to take root, it turns to lust. I've learned we need to periodically reset the speed of our clock, because the best love is slow. Like an afternoon passed in the rear of Darvill's Bookstore, sipping tea and coffee and thumbing through volumes of books we never take time to read.

We came here to slow down, to sit by a fire and read. To rekindle a flame that was struggling to stay lit at the speeds we travel. Snuggled on the porch of our cottage, we watched the sun reluctantly become day. Morning mist draped low below the pines, then vanished like Indian whispers. It was late November and a cold front moved in. There would be a storm behind it.

Our only agenda was to explore the island. A sightseeing trip took us by the jumping cliffs of Cascade Lake in Moran State Park on our way to Mount Constitution, the highest point on the island. Seen from below cedars, atop the old stone fort, the view is a great blue sea speckled with countless forested islands outlined with beaches of rocks and bleached driftwood. Throughout the sound, ferries are in constant motion. They beach themselves with mouths agape. They are mechanized basking whales inhaling cars and people and spitting them like Jonah onto dry land.

Land in the Salish is shaped by wind and waves and the destructive beauty of time. Waters of long winters seek to reclaim the islands, but they remain. Broken and jagged, whittled to rock and pine, surrounded, making their last stand. It's the wearing that makes them beautiful.

The rest of the day was spent walking. Romantic love is a slow exploration of a lover's heart. It's the simple questions. "Why does this song move you?" Or "What do you like about chai tea or wild mushrooms or the mix of trees that edge the meadow?" In knowing what she loves about these things, I learn about secret islands untraveled by anyone but me. In a crowded and charted world, these are the only undiscovered places left. The earth was created and meant to be subdued. Our hearts and minds are as vast as the image of God.

We walked an edged path where pines cast shadows on water. A base drum builds on downbeats of tidal surges, and strings appear in rushes of wind whistling through reeds. Melodies arise in calls of arctic tern and the distant loon, harmonized with deep bellows of migrating whales and soprano weeping of an eagle. The sea is an ancient love, and ours seems young in comparison. But as the nature song builds, it crescendos through our hearts and in our souls, where our love is made eternal with the water.

In a world populated by billions of people, we chose each other. In sickness or health, we chose each other. When work has gone well or badly, we chose each other. With kids and school and sports and craziness of life, we chose each other. With temptation and options, we chose each other. Our choices led to this late-fall walk in Eastsound village on Orcas Island.

Past the village our walk ends at a hand-hewn fence rising from wild grasses and overlooking a bay crowded with wooden boats anchored deeply enough to weather the coming storm. All is quiet except sounds of outgoing tide and poetry of sea birds. My wife wraps her arms around me to protect us from the cold. I'm safely anchored. Our love is deep November. Warm fires and slow walks ensure the safe passage of winter.

PARK CITY
UTAH

Alpine slide at Olympic training center

(80) (189)

Hugo Coffee & visitors center. Dogs welcome!

(224)

(248)

DOWNTOWN PARK CITY
- Atticus Coffee, books & teahouse
- High West Distillery & saloon- also great burgers
- Ski in Ski out pizza at Davanza's

Canyons Village ski resort at Park City

Park City Mountain ski Resort

✱ Washington School House Hotel -If I sell enough books, I'm taking my wife here

(224)

To Salt Lake City

(80)

(224)

(248)

Park City

(190)

(222)

Jordanelle Reservoir

(32)

Alta & Snowbird ski Resorts in Cottonwood Canyon

Good beginner fly fishing at bunny farm

Heber City

(113)

My favorite fishing guide in Utah is Justin Harding with Utah Pro Fly Fishing. Contact him for guide services, and you won't pay unless you catch a fish

Deer Creek Reservoir

(92)

Live music, saloon art workshops great food and more!

We once spent an anniversary sleeping in our van in the parking lot... was still one of the best nights ever.

→ Sundance Resort

0   6   12

MILES

←To Provo

Provo River Great Tailwater fishery

Watch for Wallsburg Summer rafters

TIMPANOGOS MOUNTAINS

29

Zen and the Art of Vanagon Maintenance, Part III

Park City, Utah

've become friends with my van mechanics. Like any relationship, it's a result of time spent together. They know a lot about my hoses and belts, and I know when they walk their basset hounds at the park. I see them en route to Little League games where I also see my friend Scott, who, like me, drives a VW van. But unlike me, Scott is competent when it comes to doing his own auto-repair work. Our kids play on two different baseball fields so we meet between outfields to discuss how driving a Volkswagen Westfalia is like a relationship with a temperamental lover. Hot. Cold. Expensive. I've had several (vans, not lovers), and the key to survival is learning the cues.

VW vans speak through all the senses. You learn to listen for groans of belts or rattling in the engine. You learn to feel the subtle vibrations of the drive train and the sweet smell of burning coolant or the acridness of engine oil. Beyond all this a sixth sense develops. The van puts out vibes, like emotions, and they like to keep you guessing.

Over a long stretch of highway, the van will all of a sudden undergo a change of mood. If you ask what's wrong, it will say, *Nothing, I'm fine.* But you know it's really saying, *Did you just look at that other van?* It never tells you exactly how it feels, but after enough breakdowns you learn to figure it out.

The plan was to reach Park City, Utah, by sunset. It's a family favorite, used as a starting point of adventure or a place to wind down after a long trip. Cresting the grade I knew something was wrong. The mood had changed. Gauges on the dash registered that all was well, but they're only good for identifying problems after they are problems. Like a thermometer confirms a fever after the aching and nausea. I drove along a knife's edge. On one side was zen and passing scenes of America. On the other a constant feeling of impending disaster.

"Are you freakin' kidding me?!"

The familiar buzzer blew with pent-up aggression. Then came smoke and engine shuddering and cussing and pulling to the side of the highway. I kicked at the gravelly dirt and the broken glass littered along the shoulder. Again my family was stuck. Again I had no idea how to fix what had gone wrong. Again I struggled with thoughts that I'm not a man because I can't fix an engine.

We have developed muscle memory for breakdowns, and everybody began the routine. Clear the back so I could stare blankly at the engine; get out snacks because we might be there awhile. The van lost fluid, which was easy to replace, but I didn't know why it was leaking. The engine cooled, and the van made it to a cheap hotel where the kids swam and I called Scott. He was raised in New Hampshire, making him an advocate for friends looking after each other. He also does squats at the gym. He asked for symptoms and responded with a reassuring level of confidence.

"Rog, you can fix this. I'll coach you through it."

He told me I'd need another hand, so I recruited my older son, and we moved the van to a spot under a streetlamp. I drove the front wheels up on the curb so the highest point of the van was in front.

"Rog, there's air in the coolant lines so the radiator isn't working efficiently. That's why it overheated on the grade."

"Yep, that's totally what I thought."

"All you have to do is bleed your radiator."

"Cool. Simple. The radiator's up front, right?"

I didn't believe I had what it took to fix it. Still I removed the grill as instructed and found the radiator and the bolt that controls the bleeder. My son held the gas pedal at a constant 2,000 rpm while I twisted the bolt.

It neared midnight and the air was still hot. Sweat smeared with dirt as we wiped our foreheads. Something happened with the bolt. It bubbled with released air and coolant oozed out. Scott told me to tighten the bolt and to top off the coolant in the reservoir first and then the overflow. My son and I worked under pale streetlight to put everything back together.

"Congrats, Rog. You did it. Good night."

I had succeeded in doing something I had always wanted to do and never thought I would. Something my dad was going to teach me but died before he could.

My son gave me a high five, and we walked across the street to buy root beers at the gas station. We drank them under neon lights, our hands black with engine grease. I put my arm around my son and smiled when he beamed with pride in our accomplishment, and then I looked the other way. I didn't want him to see me cry.

The winds shifted. Cool air descended from the mountains. In the morning we continued to Park City.

We entered Park City past a large American flag waving from a white barn and found ourselves along narrow Main Street, where the town smelled of evergreens. I felt lighter in the thin air. Warmer in purer sun.

We arrived in deep summer, but at that elevation there's always a hint of autumn. We browsed local shops and found our way into Atticus Coffee and Teahouse (and books), where we spent the afternoon. The store was named after a character in *To Kill a Mockingbird,* and though there was a literary quality to the store, it felt more like being invited into a story. Our family came alive in the pages.

Park City is nestled in a fold between mountains patterned with wide ski runs that in summer are filled with mountain bikes and alpine slides. Activity draws you up and in, and soon you are doing things you always wanted to do, being who you always wanted to be. The town is a master of reinvention. It started as a mining camp, and when other silver mines shut down, Park City became the largest producer of silver in the country. When mining faded, the town reinvented itself as a winter ski destination (eventually hosting the 2002 Winter Olympics). The Olympic winter training center is still there, and my boys loved watching ski jumpers practice twists and flips and thirty-foot airs into a massive landing pool. After that we rode an alpine slide that felt like a bobsled. I don't know how fast we traveled, but according to my younger son, he would have won gold.

Park City is now a modern recreation destination, but bones of the mining town remain. More than sixty Victorian buildings are listed on the National Register of Historic Places. They now house world-class restaurants and bars and residences. After one hundred years without a legal distillery, High West Distillery and Saloon, a ski-in bar, is bringing back the art of crafted spirits that once warmed miners through long winter nights. Utah is the most underrated state in the country. Park City is its crown jewel.

East of town the Provo River winds languidly through Heber Valley, in an area known as Utah's Little Switzerland. It's a ribbon of blue flowing through a lush landscape of green, always in view of snow-covered mountains of the Wasatch Range and always near the produce of local organic farms. The middle section of the Provo River is a tailwater fishery flowing between two reservoirs. It's known for prolific hatches and record brown trout. Even in August the water ran gin clear and cold, pressing tight against our waders.

My older son took the head of the hole we fished. I still like him to fish upstream so if he falls I can fetch him out. He'll soon be finding his own holes, and I worry incessantly about that. My younger son and I took the tail of the hole where a swifter current created a feeding lane next to a slower current.

"Daddy, where are the fish?"

I point to a place between the currents. "Right there, Son."

"Can you see them?"

"No, I can't see them."

"Then how do you know a fish is there?"

Whether it's about fishing or the art of Vanagon maintenance or the truth behind the stars, a father can teach only what he comes by honestly. I know because of the time I've spent in the flow of rivers. I've studied the water. What's on the surface is not always the truth of what's below. It is only a clue. But I know truth. I've sought it like hidden treasures. I know trout like to hold in stiller water while keeping an eye on food flowing in faster currents. I know 90 percent of a trout's feeding takes place below the surface. Still, knowing what I know, we fish by faith.

"What if we don't catch anything?"

"Then we'll try something else."

My son was tense. I leaned into him with my chin above his right shoulder so he could hear my instruction. He relaxed when I spoke of the ways of the river. I want him to remember his father's voice. I placed my left hand on his shoulder and reached gently around his body with my right, holding his hand as we gripped the fly rod together. We slowly raised the rod tip and in a quick motion made a back cast, keeping the line above the bushes behind us, then paused a beat and made a forward cast, line looping over itself, extending above the water. The nymph landed upstream. We drifted it down and nothing happened, so we repeated the motion. My son had doubts about the hole and wanted to move on. I knew there was a trout and told him it wasn't time to leave. On the next drift the indicator twitched then jerked below the surface.

"Set the hook!"

The rod looked like an upside-down U with the tip following the motion of the fish. The fish bolted upstream. The line tightened and the reel whirred against the fast clicking of the drag.

"Daddy! Daddy!"

"You know what to do, buddy."

He followed my instruction, keeping the rod up and maintaining a tight line. The fish leaped to reveal bright orange spots separating the lighter underbelly with swirls of darker browns on top. Water droplets circled in slow motion against reflected blues of bright skies bordered by oaks and cottonwoods. The rod pulsed with the raw energy of creation, and the energy was transferred from fish to line to rod to arm to the soul of a young boy in the process of becoming a man. The fish tired. My son reeled it in and with wetted hands cradled the tail with one hand while holding below the body with the other. The fish spanned wider than his chest puffed with pride.

He released the brown trout, and it darted into a deep hole. My son looked at me and smiled. In that moment he felt alive. In that moment I was his hero.

$$\times$$

There is so little time to instruct our children. We start with what we know. A father's best teaching comes from his deepest wounds. There are wounds I carry that won't heal because I keep picking at the scabs. But a man is not defined by his knowledge of an engine. A man is defined by what he does when his family is stuck on the road.

Some things I can't teach. I take my boys fishing because some lessons can be taught only by the river. I'm limited, so I have supplemented their instruction with the great teachers of the West: the Provo River, Rock Creek, the Bighorn, the Yellowstone. Below the currents of these rivers is truth sourced from watersheds of time. For when the earth was void and darkness covered the deep, the Spirit of God moved upon the waters.

I'm not my kids' hero because I can fix a van engine or because I can close a big business deal. I'm their hero because I stand in the water with them. I teach what I know and am honest about what I don't. I humble myself to call for help. I think. I pray. And I fight like hell to keep them on the road. That is fatherhood.

Before leaving Park City we returned to Atticus Coffee and Teahouse to purchase *To Kill a Mockingbird*. I was reminded that Atticus Finch wasn't good at a lot of things, but where it mattered, such as character and courage, he was a deep well. My boys will soon be teenagers. They're passing from one stage of life to the next, which means I am too. Soon they'll outgrow our van. They'll take their own road trips and discover their own highways. I panic at the thought of this. But when they do go, I hope they remember the breakdowns and time spent along desolate highways and a father who, with all his faults and limitations, used every resource he had and never gave up until they got back on the road.

Until then there's much to explore. I made sure the kids were buckled and closed the van door with confidence. Circling to the driver's side, I gave the van a pat on the nose and said a little prayer, and we continued our journey.

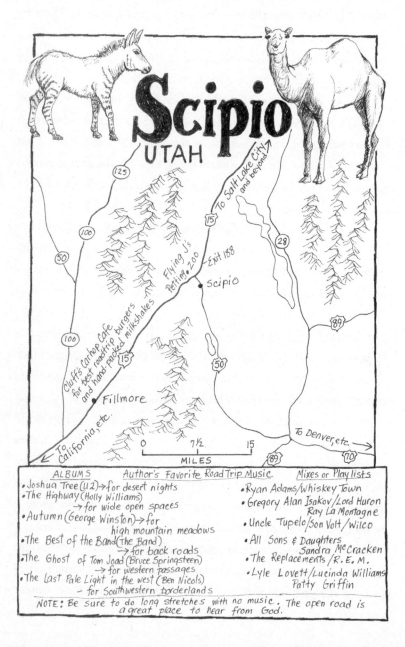

Scipio
UTAH

125

100

50

To Salt Lake City and beyond→

15

28

Flying J's Petting Zoo · —Exit 188

• Scipio

100

15

50

89

Cluff's Carhop Cafe for best roadtrip burgers and hand-packed milkshakes

• Fillmore

To California, etc. ←

To Denver, etc. →

| 0 | 7½ | 15 |
MILES

89

70

ALBUMS   _Author's Favorite Road Trip Music_   Mixes or Playlists

- Joshua Tree (U2)→for desert nights
- The Highway (Holly Williams)
    → for wide open spaces
- Autumn (George Winston)→for
    high mountain meadows
- The Best of the Band (The Band)
    → for back roads
- The Ghost of Tom Joad (Bruce Springsteen)
    → for western passages
- The Last Pale Light in the West (Ben Nicols)
    - for Southwestern borderlands

- Ryan Adams/Whiskey Town
- Gregory Alan Isakov/Lord Huron
    Ray La Montagne
- Uncle Tupelo/Son Volt/Wilco
- All Sons & Daughters
    Sandra McCracken
- The Replacements / R.E.M.
- Lyle Lovett/Lucinda Williams
    Patty Griffin

NOTE: Be sure to do long stretches with no music. The open road is a great place to hear from God.

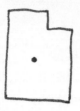

30

A Place Between Places

Scipio, Utah

We have camped all over the West and as a result have slept in the most beautiful places our great country has to offer. We've awakened to pine trees and rivers and waterfalls, mountains marked with glaciers and aspens, and deserts so vast you'd think the earth might be flat after all. We've also awakened in truck stops. Navigation can be difficult through the night with nothing more than a GPS, a smartphone, travel apps, a stack of AAA maps, a portable Wi-Fi, and extra gas and provisions. When we can't reach a campground until the following day, a twenty-four-hour Flying J parking lot serves the purpose. It's way better than a Walmart. That's not camping.

"Which way you headed, hon?"

Implied in the question was *here* could not be where we were headed. The convenience-store employee waited patiently for my answer. I had to think for a minute. My mind was foggy, having had only a few hours of sleep between sounds of trucks and truckers and PA-system announcements of store specials.

"South. Home. In California."

"I ain't been to Californ-I-A. In fact, I ain't been far from here."

I looked bleary-eyed out the store window and didn't see anything indicating where "here" was or even that there was a "here" at all.

"Where are we?"

"Sir, you are in Scipio, Utah." She was a morning person. "I've had customers from all over the country. Heck, they come from all over the world."

She described in great detail the many places her customers had been and the wonderful sights they'd seen and the delicious food they'd eaten. She herself had once taken a bus to Salt Lake City, but she couldn't remember that trip very well.

"Do you come in often? If you do, one of these twenty-four-ounce refillable coffee mugs might suit you best."

She held it up. It looked like a bucket.

"Our coffee goes real good with cinnamon rolls."

There were "fresh baked" cinnamon rolls on display near the croissant-wrapped sausage bites and bagged powder-sugar doughnuts. The Dairy Queen that occupied the other half of the travel plaza had not yet opened for business. The convenience store had every packaged food item you could hope for, and the bathrooms were the cleanest I'd seen anywhere. I thought we may spend our next vacation camping at a series of Flying Js. I paid for the coffee and cinnamon rolls.

"We also have a petting zoo. It opens in a few hours. Your kids will love it!"

I was tempted to wait.

As my family slept I drank coffee and ate warm cinnamon rolls and watched the sun rise through a gap between mountains far to the east. Our new Australian shepherd puppy curled in my lap. My wife named the dog Reese, after her favorite actress, but our boys are convinced she's named after Reese's Peanut Butter Cups, also my wife's favorite. Reese had grown much in the year we'd had her, but her teeth still retained their puppy sharpness as she licked sugar residue from my fingers.

The breeder warned us about how smart Aussies are. I've also learned that if she looks guilty, she is. When I find her in the bedroom, she glances at me sideways, avoiding direct eye contact. Her nose stoops toward the ground and her ears cock back when I ask, "What did you do?" She then uses a diversionary tactic and leads me to her leash for a walk. It's only later that I find the half-eaten roast beef sandwich.

I fell fast in love with Reese. The love came fast because it didn't start at zero. I still missed our golden retriever, Logan. But my love for him was not missing. He stretched my heart wider with love. When we got Reese, that love found its way home. Though it was intended for something different, it adapted. Love grows and adapts and becomes more perfect over time. If we let it, it makes us more perfect too.

I prayed for that kind of love for my wife and my boys. My sons were changing, transitioning from boyhood to adolescence. I didn't want this change. Partially because I knew the teenage years would come with more cool than cuddles, but mostly I didn't want it to happen because I didn't want to give the sex talk.

In California the public schools teach reproduction and sex education in the fifth grade. Most child-development experts will say parents should talk to their kids about sex even before that. Since I'm the father of two boys, the responsibility for giving "the talk" falls squarely in my area of responsibility. I wasn't looking forward to my sons' loss of innocence. Also, talking about erections is awkward.

I prayed for the transition my boys faced and for wisdom in how to father them. I prayed I would have the courage to do the right things when the right moments arrived.

The descending breeze was cool, and sagebrush smelled sweet in the sunrise. It hadn't rained, but there was wetness in the air. With Reese in my lap and my family asleep, the world felt at peace.

X

There was a time I was too consumed by work to take these trips. I rationalized it by saying we needed to save the money. I was doing ministry. The boys needed to see what hard work looked like. These were all true. Equally true was that time was slipping away and we couldn't get it back. Now we do whatever we have to do in order to take our boys on adventures, because in the blink of an eye they will be men.

I walked Reese to the other end of the travel plaza. Sure enough, there was a camel lying in the dirt against a chain-link fence. Reese barked. She tried to get the camel to play, but the camel rolled its eyes, not bothering to move. Other than the random collection of animals, nothing was visible in any direction.

To the east was Colorado. To the west was Nevada and Highway 50, the Loneliest Road in America. North were the states we had just visited: Montana, Wyoming, Idaho. And south was California and home.

Scipio is a place between places. Not a destination, but somewhere to stop as you're traveling through. I love the grand destinations, but I've come to realize this is where most of life is lived. Life is Tuesdays and Thursdays. It's peanut-butter sandwiches and fretting about the sex talk. As much as I want my life to be like wild elk and eagles and wolves, it's more like a penned-in camel at a petting zoo. Our summer adventures were ending, and soon we'd be back in our routines of work and school and fighting about bedtime. But it would be different.

Travel is a passage and we are made different through the passing. Though life can seem random as a camel at a gas station, with enough randomness it can also seem purposeful. God is always trying to get our attention. He wants to tell us He's here and He loves us. Sometimes He wants to nudge us in a different direction—or in any direction at all. I've visited the great cathedrals as well as modern churches. Sometimes I feel God there, sometimes I don't. But the more I travel off the map, the more I know He's near. The Wild is God's scent. The deeper we travel into it, the more we'll smell His presence. The farther we travel up, the more we'll see His evidence. One day our search will end and then blood will mix with water and our story will be made complete. I hear God better in the lost places, where no one else tampers with His voice.

The boys woke up and walked around the parking lot. They got excited when they saw the petting zoo.

"Look! I see asses!"

"Don't say that word."

"Why? It's in the Bible."

"Where? Where is it in the Bible?"

"I don't know. You said it was."

"Well, it doesn't matter. Those aren't asses anyway."

"What are they then?"

"They're zonkeys."

Minds were blown. The animals had the distinct look and quirky movements of a donkey but with zebra stripes. They paced a bit, then settled along the edge of the pen with striped necks hanging over the fence.

"How are zonkeys made?"

This was my opportunity. I'd been practicing my talk and developing simple hand signals to represent things such as erections and how babies are made. It was like a finger-puppet sex show. My wife and I already had agreed this was the summer to have the talk, so when my son asked about the zonkey, my wife gave me the look. It was such an easy layup. Crossing a zebra with a donkey was the perfect intro.

I cleared my throat. "Well . . ." More throat clearing.

I had everybody's attention. They were on the edge of their seats waiting to hear how zonkeys come into the world.

"Well. That's how God made them."

I could tell there would be follow-up questions so I diverted.

"Hey! Over there! Look at those chickens on a Ferris wheel."

31

The Meaning of Highways

Marfa and Big Bend National Park, Texas

've been listening to my father's music.

Eventually we lose the voices that meant the most to us. They drown in the noise or in death or in other voices, or they just fade away. I have no memory of the sound of my father, but his voice comes back to me in his music. When I hear the voices of Don Henley or Glenn Frey from the Eagles, or Levon Helm from The Band, I can see my dad singing in the cab of his beat-up truck, full of joy, full of life, with background vocals of a laboring Chevy engine and rambling sounds of the highway. His voice comes back to me in that space on the highway, after the guitar solo, when the song returns home.

I am the last of the men in my father's line, keeping it true until one day my boys become men. Our history has been written by the road. Some of that history has been lost. I've gone to West Texas to search the highway for clues. I went first, before my boys were born, to the Panhandle to look for any remaining churches started by my great-grandfather and to drive the roads that led him and my grandfather to travel west. I hoped for a discovery that would help me navigate roads ahead. Marriage. Kids. Career. Life. Death. Not all searches are about answers.

I recently returned to West Texas solely because I was drawn there. If the first trip was a search for who I am, the second was a search for who I'd become. I began in the groggy twilight, no one on the road except semitrailers with oversized white boxes that in morning light looked like sails. The gravity of the sunrise pulled me in, my foot heavy on the gas. With windows down I awoke to the coal-tar smells of the creosote bush. It was too early for music, yet highway music played. The swirl of rolling tires against grooved asphalt and the refrain in the wind of passing semitrailers blown by their highway sails.

I thought about the men I follow and their urge for open roads and how men throughout history have succumbed to the same urge. There is something embedded in us that draws us to the horizon. We are not entirely at home here. So we look beyond the oceans and deserts and mountains to the stars, and we wonder why. It's the distant wind that catches our face in the breeze and we breathe it deep through our nostrils and it smells of freedom and we know it is freedom we seek.

West Texas is a land of long, dusty roads between sparsely populated towns with banners celebrating victories of six-man football teams. I stopped at a saloon in Marfa. The entry was lit by an old streetlamp and a red neon sign spelling BEER. Inside, dim lights hung from slow-spinning fans anchored to an uneven ceiling. The saloon's plywood walls were covered in beer signs and antlers. In one corner sat a busted-up piano that looked like it had been found in the desert beneath circling crows. Playing on a small stage in the other corner was a local band with a slide guitar carrying the haunting melodies of surrounding landscapes. With the exception of a few people playing pool in the back, the crowd gathered around the bar.

The attire for the evening was mostly denim and boots and creased trucker hats or cowboy hats. I sat next to a tall, skinny man in a black cowboy hat and ordered a can of Shiner Bock beer. The man next to me had a scar on his face. It looked like the kind of scar you didn't ask questions about.

"What brings you to town?" His voice had a rasp, but his eyes and grin were friendly. He rolled a cigarette as I spoke.

"I'm looking for a place to get lost."

He gave me an inquisitive look suggesting most people who came through these parts already were.

"What kind of car you drivin'?

"A Toyota, I think. It's a rental."

He licked and pinched the edge of the rolling paper, then placed the cigarette between his teeth. "Know the difference between a jeep and a rental?"

The cigarette came alive with a match. He took a drag, blew smoke from the corner of his mouth, and continued. "You can drive a rental anywhere."

I laughed and tilted my can toward him before taking a drink. I'm convinced he had told the same joke many times before, but he laughed as if it were the first time. He gave me directions for a drive into Big Bend National Park.

"It sits on the border of Mexico, along the Rio Grande, though 'round here we call it the Río Bravo. I think you'll find what you're looking for there."

A pack of dogs roamed through the bar in a way that said it wasn't their first time. They stopped by our stools to say hello, then exited to the patio.

"Those your dogs?"

"Naw, they're just town mutts. I like 'em so I let 'em roam around. Hell, some days there are more dogs than people at this bar."

$$\times$$

The patio was made of crushed gravel, and along the fence sat neatly stacked cords of split oak. Christmas lights and neon signs lit a second, outdoor bar facing a rusted traffic signal that changed from green to yellow to red, though nobody paid attention. Several bonfires were ablaze and around one gathered a group that didn't fit. They had hats, like the rest, but their hats lacked the conviction of brims or creases, and their clothing went together in a way that suggested thought. They didn't drink from cans. I asked one of the guys how he found himself in Marfa, and he said he came for the art, but his words lacked conviction too. We were three hours from the nearest airport; he was from Chicago, the others had come from New York, and he couldn't tell me much about the art.

Against any logic, Marfa has become an international destination for modern art. I tried to get into a gallery that exhibited Andy Warhol's *The Last Supper* but the gallery was closed. I lay on the sidewalk to see the painting from under the paper that blocked the view. I could see several paintings, including the *The Last Supper.* They were all remarkable, so I stayed prone on the sidewalk for a bit, taking it in. People with uncreased hats walked around me en route to various buildings remodeled with a stunning mix of prairie and modern influences. The buildings were beautiful. I tried to gain admission to various galleries, but they were either closed or just closed to me, with no indication of when they would open. Marfa supposedly has world-class art everywhere, but I had to take the word of other people.

In an unlit alley behind the bar was a taco trailer with a sign that said to go back to the bar and ask for Ted. Ted's hat was creased, so we got off to a great start. The trailer was similar to ones I've seen at every modern street fair, only it was leveled with the aid of concrete blocks. I asked Ted what kind of tacos he had.

"*Carne*. Maybe *pollo*."

I stood at the door of the trailer with my back to the alley. As Ted cooked I asked how he felt about the influx of out-of-town art folks.

"This town used to be dead. For a while people came for the ghost lights; now they come for the art. I don't care why people come as long as they like tacos."

The following morning the town was again shut down. I went to the Frama coffee shop at the Tumbleweed Laundry, then had breakfast at Marfa Burrito near a collection of vintage travel trailers at El Cosmico. I judge towns based on their coffee and Mexican food, and this standard of measure has never failed me. In both cases Marfa scored off the chart. I came here to see about the fuss over the art, which was a bust for me. But I was falling in love with the town for other reasons. In spite of outside pressures, Marfa hangs on to West Texas roots. The town is confident enough in who it is to also be comfortable being all things to all people. That idea seemed important, but I couldn't finish my thought. Instead I headed to Mexico.

The land of West Texas is big and honest. On and on it stretches. The distance swallows time, with miles between miles. Mountains rise from nothing, looking more like shadows. They are ghosts haunting a flat land.

After receiving directions to Big Bend, I asked the man in the black hat why people came to Marfa.

"I don't know why these people are here." The thought was unfinished. He took a drag of his hand-rolled cigarette and paused, then added, "Hell, I doubt they know either."

We are all searching for something. There's a map of the world leading to places such as Marfa, Texas, and when we get there it directs us to the right galleries and the right people and the right tacos. But no matter how good the tacos are, we're still hungry the next morning.

Next that map will direct inward to needs and wants and pleasures. Those too will be fulfilled and still there will be the longing. Then like the New Yorkers visiting Marfa, we'll find the place we're looking for and still will be lost.

I followed a map to the north bank of the Río Bravo where I thought maybe I was lost. This was the border river, the Rio Grande, separating the United States and Mexico, but water flowed at a trickle. On the other side a young boy, about the age of my own, struggled to wash a broken toy in the river. In ten strides I could have crossed to help him while barely getting my shorts wet. We exchanged a glance and I waved, and he walked home to crude poverty. At about this time my boys would be leaving school to walk to a beautiful home I sometimes think of as too small. There was a trail through a thicket that led to a village, and the boy stopped before entering. He looked back to the river. He was drawn to the water. He was close enough I could tell his hair was brown and his eyes looked brown too. It's a thin line that divides us.

Continuing through the dirt and scrub brush, into the vast expanse of Big Bend National Park, I wanted to think vast thoughts. Something metaphysical, making sense of poverty and the purpose in places we are born. I tried, but my thoughts were ordinary. Kids and work, then a skit I once saw on *Saturday Night Live*. I tried again. There was a cloud that looked like a horse jumping over a mountain. I thought about how hard that would be for a real horse.

I want to believe I'm a noble adventurer who can go on forever, but I'm not. On the nation's southern border, I missed my wife and my boys and my dog. I wanted Snapper Jack's tacos and Beacon coffee. The stars of my compass turned me west, past the great deserts and high mountains to the edge of the Pacific where fires of four small souls warmed its shore. This is who I am and that's my adventure. I hadn't been lost; I'd been looking at the wrong map.

$$\times$$

Some searches are only about the search. They reveal something about who we are or who we are meant to be. The longing for beauty tells us we were made for beauty. The longing to share a campfire with someone we love, or are beginning to love, tells us we were made for love. The longing itself tells us there is something, or someone, that draws our hearts.

So the search grabs hold and we can't explain why. It comes on like a sickness, and the only cure is to pack some maps and rations and go. We are not made for the cages we've erected around ourselves. We are meant for freedom. Where trees and mountaintops point to the stars and where canyons echo and waters cool and where wind is scrubbed clean by prairie grass. Those are the lost places where we go to find God.

The winds came strong on the road from Big Bend. I stopped to fuel the car. Tumbleweeds twirled across the highway. It was wind that darkened the sky with dust, eventually leading my great-grandfather and grandfather west. The winds blow still over bluebonnets and blackfoot daisies. Some say the winds of West Texas carry omens. I turned my face into its sharpness, then returned to the highway.

Highways have changed in time, from game trails to Indian trails to wagon trails to what we travel today. But the meaning of highways remains the same. They are a hope or an escape, depending on which way you travel. They connect us to our past and to our future and to and from lost places. The highways are how we search and how we return home.

On the long winds of West Texas, I drove my grandfather's highways pointed to the Pacific. I'm not sure it was an omen, but I felt something in the wind. Peace and purpose, certain as the land.

I turned up my father's music, then put one hand on the wheel and the other out the window. Yellow dotted lines faded into the west like an unfinished thought.

Acknowledgments

At the heart of this book lies a love letter to the outdoors. As such, I'd like to begin by thanking those who dedicate their lives to protecting these sacred places. In my life, as with countless others, our National Parks and wildernesses are the cathedrals where I most encounter God. These lands need and deserve our protection. For those of us who believe this world was in some way created, the way we treat creation is a reflection of our view of the Creator. For those who believe the world began by other means, the love of our land is a common grace in which we can stand together, so by our collective efforts every soul can look up and ask the questions that make us human. From where did I come? Where am I going? What is my purpose in between?

Every (good) book is a team effort. I'd like to thank my publishing team for believing in this project and pushing me to produce something better than I thought I could. Alex Field, Andrew Stoddard, Pam Shoup, Douglas Mann, and everybody else at WaterBrook, this book would not exist without you. For any of you who wished this book didn't exist, their office is in Colorado Springs, CO.

I write around. Though I've worked on this book in over five states and a couple of countries, I'd like to thank some places in my hometown for putting up with days upon days of me writing in the corner of their shops. Kay's Coffee Shop and Beacon Coffee—you have been gracious hosts, counselors, and providers of the fuel needed to write, day in and out. And when coffee wasn't enough, thanks go to Made West and Topa Topa breweries for the afternoon sessions (though there were days I wished you were open earlier).

Perhaps the greatest contributors to our successes (or failures) in life are the friends we travel with. In this regard I've been blessed beyond the space afforded to write about it. I'd like to thank Chuck Scherrei, who journeyed with me in this effort—from first hearing the idea on a fishing trip years ago, to reading every iteration in between, and ultimately for saving Chapter 4. I'd also like to thank two of the finest men I know, Greg Bayless and Brady Jones, for the countless miles we've traveled together. I'm a better version of myself because of time spent with you. Lastly, there's a place on the banks of the Bighorn River in Montana where part of my heart resides. I'd like to extend a special thanks to Brian Carpenter and the Refuge Foundation for providing me space to renew, reflect, and pull this book together. Also for helping me catch trout. Lots and lots of them.

When I think of what I'm most grateful for, two things come to mind. First is the freedom that comes from walking with God in places He created. The second is my family. A huge THANK YOU goes out to my mom, Elain Thompson, who contributed all the artwork and maps for this book. The only thing greater than the fun it was to work together is my love for you. I am particularly grateful for my sons, Austin and Hayden. I am so delighted with each of you, and I love you with all the pride of a father's heart. Finally, nothing would be possible without my one true love, Melissa. Thank you for saying yes to me and to every adventure we've had together. There could be no better partner. By the way, I have a new idea . . .